A MARINE IN THE GREAT WAR

A MARINE IN THE GREAT WAR

J. A. Brough

Book Guild Publishing
Sussex, England

First published in Great Britain in 2012 by
The Book Guild Ltd
Pavilion View
19 New Road
Brighton, BN1 1UF

Typesetting in Garamond by
Norman Tilley Graphics Ltd, Northampton

Printed and bound in Great Britain by
CPI Group (UK) Ltd, Croydon, CR0 4YY

A catalogue record for this book is available from
The British Library.

ISBN 978 1 84624 742 2

Dedicated to my brother Michael

Contents

Acknowledgements

I wish to record my special thanks to Len Sellers of Leigh-on-Sea for generously giving me carte blanche to quote from his *RND* publications; my thanks as well to Peter Hart, co-author of *Defeat at Gallipoli*, who kindly permitted me to make use of his book, in particular Chapter 19 for a description of the conditions on Cape Helles; to the archivist and librarian of the Royal Marines Museum my thanks for guiding me in my request to quote from *Trench and Turret* by S. M. Holloway, in particular the latter's account of the Battle of Ancre.

1

Early Life

John Brough was born at Wethead on 4th March 1894, the youngest of six children of Absalom and Mary Jane Brough, née Winspear. Wethead was a small, isolated farm in Raindale on the North York Moors. It lay to the west of Newtondale; across to the east was the steep road up to the village of Levisham. The nearest hamlet, Stape, had a school where all the Brough children were educated, and a Methodist chapel which they attended.

In November 1911, tragedy struck the family with the death of the eldest son, James, following a shooting accident whilst out hunting. This occurred in Shanghai, China, where he was serving as a constable with the Shanghai Municipal Police Force. He is buried in the municipal cemetery in Shanghai.

By 1914, the farm was being run chiefly by John's surviving elder brother, Thomas; their father at 77 years of age no longer took an active part. His sister Hannah was at home looking mainly to the indoor work, baking, churning, washing, etcetera. Two other sisters – Mary, always referred to as Polly, and Jane, referred to as Jenny – were married but still lived on the North York Moors; Polly at Saintoft Cottage towards Pickering, and Jenny at Bumble Bee Farm further north near Roxby.

Wethead is mentioned by the Commission on Historical Monuments of England: Houses of the North York Moors, Wethead (Ordnance Survey map reference SE812926): 'The influence of formal planning is visible in more modest farms. Wethead, Newton, unifies the living and farming requirements of a small farm in a single building of c.1812. The stable and barn are disguised as wings of the main house, and provided with false windows.'[1] It still survives, although much altered and no longer a farm.

As Wethead was not large enough to support a second son, John had to find employment elsewhere. In early 1913, he went to work at the 100-acre Rectory Farm in the village of Levisham run by brother and sister William and Jane Keath, both unmarried. He lived in through the week, coming across from Wethead each Monday morning, usually returning home each Sunday.

William Keath

William Keath, for whom John Brough worked at Rectory Farm, Levisham, was the unmarried son of George Keath and Amelia, daughter of Robert Skelton, who was Rector of Levisham from 1818-1877.

On his father's death in 1911, William and his unmarried sister Jane took over the running of the farm. It was rented from the Rev. W. J. E. Armstrong, Rector of Levisham.

William was much involved with the local church (several times in John Brough's diary, William was 'away on church business').

His name often appears in the Levisham Churchwarden's Accounts:

18 May, 1904	Wm Keath bell-ringing	£1.0.0d[Oct-Apr]
13 Aug, 1906	Wm Keath bell-ringing	£1.0.0d[Oct-Apr]
27 Mar, 1907	Wm Keath repairing bell-rope	£0.1.0d
19 May, 1907	Wm Keath bell-ringing	£1.0.0d[Oct-Apr]
10 May, 1910	Wm Keath filling water tank & bell-ringing	£1.10.0d
May, 1911	Wm Keath -ditto-	£1.10.0d

---

[1] *Houses of the North York Moors*, Royal Commission on Historical Monuments of England, Stationery Office Books, 1987, p. 000.

Vestry meeting, Thurs, 8 Jun, 1911 – vacancy for People's Warden through lamented death of George Keath. Wm Keath elected.

May, 1912 Wm Keath filling water tank £1.10.0d
           & bell-ringing

Apr, 1914 Wm Keath re-elected People's Warden

May, 1914 Wm Keath archdeacon's visitation fee   £0.12.0d
                      churchwarden's fee   £0.10.0d
                      bell-ringing, filling water tank £1.10.0d

[He continued to be re-elected People's Warden and to receive payments for bell-ringing, water tank filling, etc. through the war years]

Feb, 1919 Purchase of 1ton 2cwts 2qtrs of coke   £2.14.2d
           Carting above to Pickering Stn   £0.05.0d
           Wm Keath leading from Levisham Stn   £0.09.9d

Vestry Meeting 7 Apr, 1920.
    Mr Wm Keath did not wish to be a candidate for People's Warden. Meeting adjourned to give time to find a candidate.
    [George Hammond was subsequently elected]

    William was still getting his annual fees for bell-ringing and attending to the water cistern up to the end of the records in 1923.

At the end of a long day's work, there was not a deal of entertainment in the unlit surroundings of Levisham. John enjoyed reading and there was a reading room in the village. He was a member of Stape Brass Band which occupied much of his leisure time – there was a band room in Levisham village as well as an old house in Raindale that the band used.

The Broughs were members of the Primitive Methodist Chapel, and the scattered farms of Raindale, including Wethead, served as venues for house meetings on a Sunday afternoon addressed by a local lay preacher. Afterwards, John would make his way up to Stape chapel for the evening service, hopefully to meet up with friends and neighbours from the dale.

There is no reference to the Horseshoe Inn, Levisham's pub, or mention of going for a drink in my father's diary; perhaps a result of his Methodist upbringing. As well, his employers at Rectory Farm, William (44 in 1914) and Jane Keath (55), were both of a strait-laced nature, much involved with church work, and probably disapproving of drink. Maybe, however, being just 20 years of age in 1914, he and his fellow farm lads would not be welcomed at the pub by the older men of the village. Or, on his weekly wage of 9/-, there was little to spare for a drink.

Another way in which he passed his time was to keep a diary. This he did assiduously, perhaps after work, sitting in the stable to record the day's events with the scant light of a candle or a paraffin lamp.

Unfortunately, his diaries for the intervening years of the First World War are missing. I understand that they were borrowed by a friend who failed to return them. This may be so, as I located a diary (for the time he was a POW in Germany) at the Royal Marine Museum, Southsea, sent to the museum by someone in 1986.

So, I have tried to tell my father's story from Raindale to Passchendaele with his own recordings of day-to-day life in 1914, a farm lad on the North York Moors, and concluding with his diary as a POW in Germany.

Without my father's diaries for the war years, I have tried to follow his likely experiences by reference to the history of the Royal Naval Division, in which he served as a Royal Marine, and to the recollections of men who served with the Royal Naval Division. Much of my information is taken from a quarterly journal *RND*, produced by Mr Len Sellers of Leigh-on-Sea, Essex, first published in June 1997. This records the history of the Royal Naval Division throughout its existence, 1914 to 1919.

Knowing in which battalion at any particular date my father was serving, I have been able to follow that battalion, and hence my father, throughout his active service. In the accounts that follow of Gallipoli and of the Western Front, a unit shown in bold type indicates that my father was with that unit at that time.

2

John Brough's Diary 1914

Sun 1st Mar

Got up about seven, did the horses. After breakfast, I got washed and dressed then sat down and had an hour's reading, then I set off for Wethead – landed up just before dinner. It was our meeting this afternoon, I stayed but Tom did not. I came over to Levisham church at night and stayed there [at Levisham]. It has been a nice fine day. Nathan [Pickering] was preacher.

Mon 2nd Mar

I did not wake up till six and thought it a bad start for Monday morning seeing I got up all last week at five. After we got all done up about the yard, William and I set off with the wagon for the sticks we got out of the West Bank Wood on Saturday. We took the young mare with us and two of the others. Got all the sticks on one load and put them down the stackyard, then got some hay in with the wagon to make up dinner-time. After dinner, William went to Pickering and I went to plough. I ploughed up to the nets with a rigg then went a few times round a throwing-out piece. I went and got my hair cut at night by Robinson's wagoner, Mr Myers. It has been a fine day and is freezing a little tonight.

Tues 3rd Mar

Did not get up till six. When we got all done up, William went to the sheep while I was ploughing. Got the piece ploughed to about four furrs and then it was dinner-time. I cannot plough any more now till the sheep get some more land cleared. After dinner, I started to thatch the straw stack, got it almost done. At night, I went over to Lockton to hear an evangelist man tell his history – my word, he had been a rum chap for drinking when he was a young man. Frank Stead went with me. It has been a fine day but cold, was inclined for rain tonight.

Wed 4th Mar

My word, it is my birthday [20 years old]. Well, I must wish myself many happy returns of the day as nobody else has done so! During the morning, we were leading manure on to the big field. We had the young horse yoked and he went very well. After dinner, we yoked the young mare and she was rather too lively – we have been using four of them. About four, we loosed out and I went to pull turnips, also helped to dig a ford for the sheep. Hannah has been over today helping Miss Keath to wash. It was wet first thing this morning but got out finer, yet it has been rather dull all day.

Thurs 5th Mar

Got up at six, did the horses then I went with William for some turnips – got three load and big ones, too – put them in the turnip house, and it was about full. After dinner, William went to Newton to get Diamond shod and I went to thresh at Robinson's. I was carrying straw and it was a long way; we put it in the barn. It came on a very nasty wet afternoon and made it a bit bad to do. Frank and I played a joke on Rickensons at night. Fine morning, damp afternoon.

Fri 6th Mar

Got up at six. After breakfast, I took two cartload of manure down to the garden and brought a load of stones back from down there for the yard as we are going to repair it round by the horse trough. I also brought one load out of the quarry. When we got that done, we went down into the cistern to see if we could find where it leaks, as it will not hold water. We mended a place where we thought the water got out – we spent the day doing such like. It has been a fine day but a most awful big wind making a merry scale in the stack-yards, but it is much calmer tonight.

Sat 7th Mar
Got up at six, did the horses then, after breakfast, I got two sets of harrows out and took them in the cart to the five-acre field and started to harrow with the straight set. It worked very well. There are a lot of brassocks [wild mustard] growing and we hope to kill some of them. I have been harrowing all day, got it done double over then took the harrows to Swallowdale. Did not get a start to use them as it was night. It has been a fine day drying the land up beautiful.

Sun 8th Mar
Got up at seven and did the horses. After breakfast, set off home. Tom was over last night with my strong boots which have been getting soled. I have not been anywhere today – I had the gramophone on a while. Tom went across to Saintoft and Hannah was at the meeting. It was a wet morning but got out fine later on. I saw a primrose today – the first I have seen this year – it had grown down the wood.

Mon 9th Mar
I had a bad attack of toothache about one so got up and stayed till four, then felt a bit better, so went to bed and slept till 7.30, so did not get to work today. I was helping Tom to lead manure and to yoke the young pony. She went very well but I think we pulled her too much, as she was not too well tonight and we had to give her a colic drink. We went to Pashby's and had a good game of dominoes. It has been a showery day and has a watery look tonight.

Tues 10th Mar
Got up about five, got some breakfast then set off to Levisham. William and I went and were pulling swedes off all morning – most people are busy with that kind of work now. After dinner, we went

and got a load of thorns and put them on the quarry top in the limekiln field, got them from Low Swallowdale hedge. It has been a fine day, is drying up again, but it was a very keen white frost last night.

Wed 11th Mar
Got up about six. After breakfast, I went to lead swedes off down the stackyard — got three big loads, all that was pulled. After dinner, we went down Swallowdale to clean up the fire sticks and it took us all afternoon. I have the toothache yet and am about tired of it now. It has been a fine day, was another frost last night.

Thurs 12th Mar
I woke up at three and my nose was bleeding so had to jump out for a handkerchief. Just when I had got nicely into bed again I had to come down as I heard the horses making a great noise, and it was old Jet which had been laid fast [got stuck]. We have been pulling turnips most of the day and shifting nets. There was a band practice tonight. It was white over with snow this morning when we got up, but it soon went away and has been a fine day. I am going to put the old mare in the box tonight.

Fri 13th Mar
I had a lot to write last night so had to scribble to get it done. I started to lead off swedes this morning, got four load. It came on wet when I was getting the third load and kept getting worse till after dinner. It faired up about three, so we had the cart and got some hay in. It is the first start of the second stack, and it is the same as the other was — half seed hay and half old land hay. I am going to the reading room for a while tonight. It has been a wet day. Mrs Anderson called as she was too late for the five train — fancy!

Sat 14th Mar
I have had toothache all week so, last night, I went and had it pulled out by Lockton blacksmith Mr Thompson. Frank went with me. It

does not ache now. We were pulling turnips and shifting nets all morning and, during the afternooon, I was leading off. We have got a good-sized heap now. It has been a rather wet day but not so bad as it looked; it was thundering during the afternoon.

Sun 15th Mar
Got up at seven, did the horses. Had to help William to get a turnip out of an old ewe's throat and the old brute bit my finger, but not seriously. After breakfast, got washed and changed and went home. I intended coming over to the church at night but did not get fit soon enough. It has been a fairly fine day but is very dark tonight and is coming on wet

Mon 16th Mar
I was going to have come over here early this morning but it was raining, so mended a puncture in my bike − and also made another as I was putting the cover on. Did that twice, so gave up the attempt. I came to Levisham later on, about nine. Came to William in the field and was pulling turnips till the rain drove us away, then we started to clean out the boxes. It faired up after dinner and I got some turnips led off (after I had finished the boxes) and also some hay in when William got back from Pickering. Wet morning, fine afternoon. I had to work in my Sunday trousers today.

Tues 17th Mar
Got up at six, did the horses and, after breakfast, started to lead away the manure we got out of the boxes yesterday. After dinner, I went and scruffled [hoed between rows] the swedes up − got them done by night, they are better to do when scruffled up. It has been a fine drying day. One of the ewes lambed during the night and both lambs were starved to death when found. Did not expect any yet but George Stead's tup got among them once.

Wed 18th Mar
Got up at the ordinary time. After breakfast, William and I started to fay corn. It was not a wet morning but came on wet afterwards

and was very nasty, but we were in shelter so did not care much. We were on flailing all day, bagged it all up fit for sowing. There was a band practice tonight, Tom came over. It has been a wet day, cold and snowy, also William heard it thundering. It is very wet on the land and is keeping people back with sowing.

Thurs 19th Mar
Got up a bit late. After breakfast, I started to lead manure out of the back ford with the wagon and three horses, only got two load before dinner. Took it into the big field which is fauf [fallow] this time. It came on wet at dinner-time and lasted a couple of hours. I got another two load after it faired up but most awful and clarty [muddy]. I have got the shed cleaned out. Have been with myself all day, and never knocked any gate-posts! It has been a rather damp day and cold.

Fri 20th Mar
I had just got cleaned out and such like when Robinson's boy came for me to go to thrash. So went, and was among the corn, but it was oats, so managed all right. We had a good half day, about 12.30 when we finished. After dinner, I took a wagon-load of turnips to Swallowdale for the hogs. We brought the sheep in last night for the first time and have got two more lambed. Our folks had a commotion last night after a stray dog was in the yard about 2 and 3 this morning. It has been a fine day.

Sat 21st Mar
Got up at six but it was a very wet morning so could not get the horses out, but we started to chop when we had got all done up, cut the cow chop before dinner and was cutting horse chop after, and also pulping. It has been wet every bit of the day. Tom Nicholson and Harriet Stead were married today, not a very nice day for the job. Frank and I had a race at night but, of course, he won. It has got out a bit better night [after a wet day it became fair in the evening].

Sun 22nd Mar
Got up at seven. Did all up then went home after breakfast. It was a lovely day. I came back at night but was too late for church. Called at Woodmansey's and was there a long time.

Mon 23rd Mar
I was pulling turnips at am and getting hay in at afternoon. William was at Pickering, did not get back till the 8 train, so I had all to do. Fine day, wet at night. I got two wagon-load of hay in by myself — and it was an awkward job.

Tues 24th Mar
I started to plough a bit more of the pond field as the sheep have got another break cleared. Was ploughing all day. Been a fine day.

Wed 25th Mar
Went to plough again and got ploughed up to the nets again, but it took me hard into the night to get it done. There was a band practice, I did a bit on the tenor. Been a fine day.

Thurs 26th Mar
I went to harrow in Swallowdale. Had three horses in the chisel-teeth harrows. It did not work very well, was very sad. It came on wet at night. I was over at Lockton — came back singing, had a bit of fun, as well.

Fri 27th Mar
I was leading turnips off at morning and putting them over the hedge into the limekiln field into a heap. After dinner, I went and was harrowing in Swallowdale. Harrowed it cross over today and it worked much better. Did not get it all done over today — got it a single over yesterday, singling it today again. Been a fine day. Dr Clayton's day.

Sat 28th Mar
I went to harrow in Swallowdale at morning. Got it finished off

except the riggs and furrs and I had them to do after dinner, and they took me much longer than I had expected. I shifted over to the pond field and did a bit there to make night up. It has been a fine day but not much wind. It has been John William Eddon's wedding today and Jane Watson of Brown Head.

Sun 29th Mar

I got up at seven and did the horses. After breakfast, I had a sit-down then went across home for dinner. Tom had been at the wedding last night and had gone over to Saintoft when he landed back this morning about seven. I came over to Levisham at night, was coming at afternoon but it came on very wet. Fine morning, wet afternoon. Miss Newlove has come to see Miss Heath today. It was a very dark night, could hardly see.

Mon 30th Mar

I was leading turnips off all day and William has been pulling. Took some into the little field and the rest just over the hedge at the quarry end where we have a heap. It was rather a dull day and a very wet night. I and Magson and Johnny Welburn were out against George Stead's cow-house when George came up and nearly pittled [urinated] on us as it was dark and he did not see us.

Tues 31st Mar

It was a stormy morning so we had the engine on and pulped some turnips and cut a bit of cow chop, also were scraping the yard up. It faired up at dinner-time and we went and led some more turnips off. There is about a dozen or so bits of rows left now, but too many by far, as we have got two big heaps – one at home and one in the field. I was at Lockton at night, went by myself, did not stay long. Fine afternoon.

Wed 1st Apr

We took some stakes up in the old cart and fenced a few gaps up in the little field hedge, then got a few fire sticks out of the old fence on the quarry top and also made a bit of wall up between Howe field and the limekiln field. After dinner, I was harrowing in the pond field, got all done that is ploughed. It works very well. Been a fine day.

Thurs 2nd Apr

We started to drill. Took our own drill to Swallowdale and dabbed a few oats in till dinner. After dinner, got John Stead's then were able to tell where we had been, as 15 rows do more than 7. We did not get it all done. William has been harrowing with lame Jet. I got a very bad mark. Hannah has been over today. Been a lovely day, grand moonlit night. I stayed a bit late to get the seed used. An old ewe died today and left two lambs. Up to now, we have lost 4 lambs and 2 ewes and a pet lamb which Strawberry got which was like dying.

Fri 3rd Apr

I have been getting up at half past five this week. I went and took some seed to the field and then started to drill. William has not been harrowing this morning. Got the field drilled then brought the drill to the top of the cow pasture, and John Stead got her as they want to put some in up there this afternoon. Georgie and Sarah came this afternoon and I gave Georgie a tune on the gramophone. I was harrowing this afternoon where William left off. Been a very fine, sunny day.

Sat 4th Apr

I got an alarm clock and a few more things from Smiths Patents yesterday but it did not alarm as well as it ought this morning. I have set it to go off at five. It is a very nice copper-coloured one with two bells. I went to finish out harrowing and, when I had got it done the same way as it is drilled — from Robinson's hedge to Stead's — I started the other way but did not get it done over. After dinner, we got the drill again and put the 5 acre in on the boak [beam for attaching horses to plough], but it took us till late as we got a bad start at dinner-time. William was harrowing with the old mare with a couple of wood harrows and was able to keep up with the drill. George has gone away again. It has been much colder today and inclined for showers at afternoon. I did not get done till nine. Had our supper at eight, and a rotten old kipper, too! I think we get worse, at least, I am rather tired of it as it happens too often — kippers and swimmers! How I and Howard used to laugh about them.

Sun 5th Apr

I did not get up till half past seven, but it was not that I wasn't awake, but I was reading a Horner's Penny Story — and it was a stormy morning, as well. I had a sit-down once I had got done up and, about dinner-time, I went home, but came back in time for church at night. There is nothing doing much at Levisham. Frank Stead is ill and we had prayers at church for him, I believe he has bronchitis or inflammation. William is going to sit up with the ewes for the first night. Jane had a lamb invalid tonight, it had been nearly starved so had to have a drop of whisky, been lambed out in the wet. Been a wet day, coming in crabbed showers with much wind.

Mon 6th Apr

I like to be here on a Monday morning best as when I have to walk from home it makes you feel tired, but another reason is this, I seldom get any breakfast when I land over. We went and cleaned a few turnips for the old ewes, and a fresh ford at morning. I also led them home after dinner. Jane went to market. I went to harrow in Swallowdale but did not finish it (I started where I left off on Saturday). It came on a wet afternoon so I was forced to leave, got almost wet through. It has been a most awful cold day with a strong wind and kept coming, this afternoon, some very heavy showers — real hurricanes while they lasted, like starving the lambs.

Tues 7th Apr

I went and finished off harrowing in Swallowdale then brought the old drill and the harrows home (put the harrows in the old cart and tied the drill behind). After dinner, we were getting hay in and it took us most of the afternoon. Tom came over at dinner-time for his seed oats and also pulled a few turnips, which William gave him, before he went back. Been a rather showery day and cold.

Wed 8th Apr

We started this morning to get the corn pike in. Just got a start on it when it came on a very nasty shower and we had to wait till it was done, then first one thing then another came to bother us, till it was turned four when we got it in. There were two great ramping loads, and a most awful lot of thistles among them. It is an awkward job for one man to pack the sheaves in the granary above the engine as the old boak is in the way. Was chopping a bit at night. There was a band practice. I was on tenor, have kept her as I am on playing her a bit now it is Tom's tenor. Showery day.

Thurs 9th Apr

I went to harrow this morning in the pond field, finished out the bit that was left to do up and down, then started cross over, and got it done by dinner. It was a bit too much turning round for three horses (as I used the chisel harrows) cross over, and only half the field at that, as the other is to plough yet. I went back during the afternoon and dragged the low end against Robinson's wall as there are a few wicks [couch grass] down there, did it three or four times over (just to the first hedge of Robinson's). It came on a wet night, also was wet at dinner-time. I was over at Lockton at night shopping.

Fri 10th Apr (Good Friday)

I thought we might have had a holiday today but no such luck. When we got all done up, we went to dig the few turnips the sheep had, it is the last lot now. Then we went to fence at the top of the quarry in the limekiln field, did not get it all done. I was over at Lockton at a Service of Song at night. Showers but very fine on the whole. Most of the boys had a holiday

Sat 11th Apr
We went to drill this morning in the pond field. Started with our own [drill] at first as John Stead's were using theirs, but Albert brought her up before we had been three times about, then I could get on – finished about four in the afternoon. Of course, we had a good dinner-hour as there is so much to do, what with one thing and another. William has the ewes to look after but he has been harrowing with the old mare today using two wood harrows. It was in grand form was the land. Fine day.

Sun 12th Apr (Easter Sunday)
Got up at half past six, did the horses. After breakfast, changed and went home. (Miss Newlove came last night.) It was our meeting. We had a good company, Polly and family are over for the weekend. We thought the Eddons were coming and we got the chairs ready for them but they went past to the moor, it caused us a lot of needless bother. I came back at night but was too late for church. Been a very fine day – fine Easter, fine harvest – let's hope it will be.

Mon 13th Apr
Got up at my usual time, half past five. Did the horses then, after breakfast, I went to plough the pond field. Set a rigg up the middle of the piece and got it rigged up by night as I have been at it all day. Fine day, rather cold and windy. Miss Jane went to market and had a stew to get off as usual. Miss Newlove does not seem to approve of her ways at all, as she told me when Jane got away while we had our dinners.

Tues 14th Apr
I again went to plough this morning and nearly got the throwing-out piece done up the hedge side, about a yard left. I had the gramophone on at night till half past ten from eight. It has been a very fine day, quite warm and sunny, like summer.

Wed 15th Apr
I went to plough again today but have not got it all ploughed yet. Took the furr up and got a nice bit done at the throwing-out piece

at the other side, but it has set as hard as the highroad itself and the old plough takes no end of holding in, there will be a lot of clots. I keep harrowing it up as much as I get ploughed every day. Been a nice warm day with a drying wind making the land clotty and hard. We had a band practice at night.

Thurs 16th Apr
I went to plough again and had an awful job to cut through it as the land was so very hard with the sheep having been on when it was wet and then drying up so sharp (it was all cracked with the sun). I started to plough the headland after dinner, got the top one done all right but could not do the bottom one − it will have to stay till it rains, it is just like a stone, you see there has been a lot of carting done on it. Miss Newlove went away this morning − she walked back, her home is at Thornton-le-Dale. Fine day. Our ewes only lamb slowly yet we are having good luck up to now except at the start, lost one since.

Fri 17th Apr
I went this morning first to harrow a bit then I went to the five-acre for the roller and started rolling the clots as there are a lot at the top end. Did it up and down. It was hard work but much faster. Did not get it quite done over before dinner so finished off after and started harrowing. Used the three-chisel harrows for most of it and the big chisel for the very rough, which is down the side where it is sown to. Did not get it all done harrowing, shall have it to finish off tomorrow. Fine day, much colder.

Sat 18th Apr to Sat 25th Apr
I have kept putting off writing my diary till I am a long way back. During the week we have had very fine weather, very hot most of the days. I drilled the piece of land in the pond field on Tuesday, sown it with oats. It was very rough and I had it to roll over again before drilling, drilled on the top of rolling. I have also had a day's quarting [ploughing across the direction of previous ploughing] in the big field on Wednesday, and William was away at Malton on the

church affair, and we had a band practice at night – broke the door open as Ben was too long in coming. On Saturday, we were rowing among the sheep and lambs, and the old lame mare foaled about the middle of the forenoon – both are getting on well, it is a colt. Miss Violet Holliday out of the dale was married on the 18th. We also led a truck of gravel off, and she takes to it well [the mare]. I was over at Lockton at night and Jack Bother, from Robinson's, and Frank went with me. I have got some stuff to clean the bike as I have taken her to pieces so that I can do it better. On Friday, we were messing about, got a dess of hay in and such like jobs. I saw a swallow on Wednesday, and heard the cuckoo on Saturday 25th. Getting up time for the week 5.15 a.m.

Sun 26th Apr
When I got all done up, I got changed and went home – got there about 12.30 as I stayed talking at Levisham. I came over again at night but was too late for church. Very fine day. Our people are well, Hannah has gone to wait on a woman at Middleton.

Mon 27th Apr
I went to Swallowdale this morning with the chain harrow and started to harrow the brassocks up, it made the ... look a bit daft yet it rubbed a lot of brassocks up. It took me all day to do it. Old Bob Addison is working at G. Stead's now. He was in Howmer today and would talk to me at the ends and bothered me a lot. Jane went to Pickering instead of William. Tom was over at dinner-time for some corn. I have been doing a bit at the bike today. Been a very fine day.

Tues 28th Apr
William and I took the wagon to the bull field for a load of thorns which G. Stead gave us out of the hedge which they have felled between our field and theirs. We took them down to Ings – left half in the Church field and the rest in the far field. We did not pull the load over but put them off where we wanted them. After dinner, I had to go to the station with Tomlinson's luggage as they are off

away and, when I got back, was gardening till night. Been a very hot day. I am thinking of going to Whitby tomorrow. I went with Francis Stead on the back lane for the pony at night as he was afraid to go by himself.

Wed 29th Apr

I went to quart at morning and have been ploughing all day. I did not get to Whitby as about dinner-time I saw there was a sea-fret [mist coming in from the sea] on up in the north. It did not reach us but I felt it falling damp as I came home at dinner-time. There was an excursion at two for Whitby, it is the Tournament of Song. As I came down I saw Thomas Robinson, and he thought that our mare would foal tonight. No one turned up for a band practice tonight, I had a tune on the tenor in the stable. It has been a cold day and rather windy, I expect we shall be having a change of weather soon. The bullock by Charlie from Robinson's came to me at night – he's not such a bad old sort though not very good-looking.

Thurs 30th Apr

Got up at half past five and, after breakfast, was off to the field, but Jane thought I had better stay as William has a cow like calving. She has gone nearly a fortnight over her time and, all day yesterday and during the night, she has never lain down, she seems to have some pain in her at times. William and I got a wagon load of hay in at morning. After dinner, we went down the garden to set potatoes. The cow started to calve about five at night but the calf had a leg back, so we got Jack Hammond to help us and, after a lot of bother, he was able to get it turned but it took us all our time to get it. I never saw such a big calf before – like one a month old – but it was dead when calved. It has been a cold day but fine. The mare has not foaled yet.

Fri 1st May

I went to plough and have been ploughing all day. The cow is not well so Jane had to go to see Blench about her. He sent a drink which we gave her tonight, she doesn't get cleansed. It has been

very cold today. William had to kill another lamb today, it had got
wool on its stomach [eaten some sheep fleece]. We eat them – the
one that he killed on Wednesday was very good – it is not like
having an infectious disease. I am thinking of going for a week's
holiday at Whitsuntide. We have not got another foal yet, but don't
[t]hink she will go very long now. I saw Robinson's had a runaway
in the little field between the lanes opposite our limekiln field.
Nothing was any worse as they had not much room to gallop far.
The same pair that always go, it is not the first time by a long way.
May gosling.

Sat 2nd May
Got up about the usual time, five, and I really have forgot what we
were busy with as I did not write it down. Went to the station at
morning for some small seeds, and got some hay and such like
during the afternoon. It had been a very keen frost last night, down
the roadside great icicles were hung just like the middle of winter,
and it was bitter cold. I think it will have damaged fruit trees. Been
a fine day but cold.

Sun 3rd May
I went home after I had got all done up and had changed. Hannah
is still away at Middleton. Tom went over to Saintoft during the
afternoon. Aunt Ann came down to see our folks. I went back to
Levisham at night. The mare had been like foaling during the afternoon and she foaled about ten or half past. We had just been looking at her before and, when we went out again after supper, she was
on the way foaling. She was a bit crabby at first but I rubbed her
mouth well with the cleanings and she looks all right. We stopped
with her all night till morning. I had a sleep on some straw for I am
a bad sitter-up. It is a filly foal.

Mon 4th May
Had not to get up this morning as I was up all night, but I felt a bit
sleepy. I and William were getting hay in during the morning and,
after dinner, we went for a cart load of sand out of Bragate Hill for

21

to mix with cement for the cistern. After that, I was getting straw in and suckling the foal and watering the mare and such like till night. She seems to be taking to it yet she is rather crabby with it at times. It has been a rather wet day.

Tues 5th May
I did not wake up very soon as I was very tired. When we had got all done up, I and William went to wall a gap up in the five-acre. It took us all morning and a part of the afternoon to do it as it was eight yards long. Then we went round the other walls putting the stones up till night. Harriet Stead had a baby today, been married six weeks. It has been a showery day, there has been thunder about.

Wed 6th May
I did not get up very early. I went to plough the pond field headland when I got all worked up. It was very hard but managed to get it done, then harrowed it up with the big chisel harrow, and made dinner-time up harrowing in the big field. After dinner, I rolled the turn to the front over the piece we are going to set potatoes on and then I started to plough till night. I have had Diamond and lame Jet, the first time she has been out since she foaled. It has been a fine day.

Thurs 7th May
I did not get up very soon. Did the horses (they take a lot of doing seeing that we have two mares with foals, three in the stable, and the pony) then, after breakfast, William and I went among the sheep for an hour or so. Then went down the Ings to fence and were fencing all day. It has been roaking [dry and misty] a good part of the day, looked very black at times but kept fine. The hedges were all full of water and made it very nasty working under them.

Fri 8th May
Got up at five, did the horses then, after breakfast, went to fence in the Church field. It was a nasty roakey morning early on but got out better later. It came on wet about three in the afternoon and kept at

it till six, we had to shelter an hour in the shed. Ben Simpson and Jack Hammond came to shelter as well. I had a practice on the tenor tonight. It is lovely down the hill for flowers of all descriptions are in full bloom.

Sat 9th May

Got up at five, did the horses. After breakfast, it came on very wet so could not do anything outside at all. Florrie Gibson has got married today today at Newton to Jim Masterman of Hartoft. We were busy siding up the granary during the morning. It was better weather after dinner so got some hay in. Got two desses [blocks of hay] in, it was very windy. I was over at Lockton at night. Been very cold today.

Sun 10th May

Did not get up till seven but, when I had got all done up, I changed and went home. It is Lockton Primitive anniversary today. I came over to it at night. Did not get inside as we were a bit late. Had a bit of good sport with some girls and got a bat over the head with the umbrella for our pains. Fine day, rather dull. Some of the Levisham boys have got into a row for letting some cows into G. Stead's seed field − John Welburn did it.

Mon 11th May

Got up as usual and, when I had got all done, I went to make some potato rows. Made them on the wall side just below the gate into the limekiln field, buggers they are, too!

Mon 1st June

I am having my holidays this week at Loftus-in-Cleveland with Mrs Booth. I did not go far till night then I went to Saltburn and arrived about half past five, the road was packed with people going to the fair. I got took in by a man selling watches and chains, pretended to put money in with the things but, when we got them, they were empty. There were round-abouts and cars and scores of other attractions, more than we get at Pickering. I had a walk on the pier right out to sea, fully a quarter of a mile. We had to pay 1d to go on, also had a penny ride up a steep rock incline railway. Harold Nicholes was with me a bit at night. Came back by train; my word, there was a crush, fit to squeeze the life out of one. Esther and Alf walked both ways, landed in just after me at twelve. Been a very fine day.

Notes on the diary

This is as far as his diary goes for 1914.

References to 'furrs' and 'riggs' and 'throwing pieces' are terms connected with the ridge and furrow method of ploughing. When preparing to plough, the first task was to measure off the 'headlands', a strip of land at each side of the field on which the horses turned, allowing maybe four or five yards from the boundary hedge. The next job was to 'set a rigg', i.e. place some sticks from the hedge in a line across the field as markers and then plough once up and down in line with the markers, the plough turning the furrows to the right to form a ridge thus 'setting the rigg'. It was then a matter of ploughing clockwise around the rigg, down one side and back up the other, ploughing as many 'furrs' (furrows) as required either side of the rigg. In larger fields there could be several 'riggs', and the land between each rigg was the 'throwing out piece' which was ploughed anti-clockwise. Finally, the headlands would be ploughed. A day's ploughing involved a great deal of walking so that it was usually the lot of one of the younger farm lads, as it was with my father at Rectory Farm.

It was necessary to follow this method of ploughing as a pair of horses needed a wide turning circle so it was not possible to plough straight back and forth across a field and, as the ploughshare was fixed, always turning the furrows to the right, this would have produced a series of ridges across the field.

Ploughing 'up to the nets' was to plough up to the moveable wire netting beyond which sheep were still on the land.

References to 'leading off' means carting away in a wagon.

24

3

The Outbreak of War

On his return to Rectory Farm after his holiday, only a few weeks remained to August and the outbreak of war.

On 17th November 1914, John took the train to York and enlisted into the Royal Marine Light Infantry. He would be away from home for over four years, during which time both his parents died (in 1917) and the family gave up Wethead. Hannah joined sister Polly and her husband, who were now living in Leeds; and his brother Tom relocated to Brotton in Cleveland.

So the Brough connection with Raindale was severed. It went back to well before his grandfather first farmed Wethead. John never returned to live on the North York Moors or to work on the land.

Some reminders of the Brough family still remain. In St John's church Newton-on-Rawcliffe, John Brough's name is inscribed on a wall plaque listing the names of the men of the parish who served in the First World War. In the graveyard of St Peter and St Paul, Pickering, is the tombstone of his grandparents, Thomas and Hannah Brough.

Likewise, there is the tombstone of his uncle, another John Brough, and his wife, Elizabeth, in the graveyard of Goathland church. In the village, a cottage still stands that this uncle, a stone-mason, built in 1878. A stone slab with initial B in the middle of the date is set into the wall of the present building.

4

The Royal Naval Division

Formed August 1914, disbanded June 1919. At the start of the First World War, there were many naval reservists – between 20,000 and 30,000 of them – for whom places at sea could not be found. Winston Churchill, who was then First Lord of the Admiralty, came up with the idea of turning them into a force to fight as soldiers. It was named the **Royal Naval Division**, and was made up of two Naval Brigades, supplemented by one Marine Brigade:

1st Royal Naval Brigade
1st Btn Drake, 2nd Btn Hawke, 3rd Btn Benbow, 4th Btn Collingwood.

2nd Royal Naval Brigade
5th Btn Nelson, 6th Btn Howe, 7th Btn Hood, 8th Btn Anson.

3rd Royal Naval Brigade (Marines)
9th Btn Portsmouth, 10th Btn Plymouth, 11th Btn Chatham, 12th Btn Deal.

The Marine Brigade was organised on traditional Army lines, but the men in the Naval Brigades, although they wore khaki, had naval cap badges and insignia, held naval ranks, and used naval terms, though few of them had ever been to sea. This strange set-up did not go down very well with the Army officers later appointed to command them.

Nevertheless, the **Royal Naval Division** became a very effective fighting unit. Winston Churchill said that the Division came to be regarded in 'the glorious company of the seven or eight most famous in the British Army'.

Some of the personalities who served with the **Royal Naval Division** were:

- Rupert Brooke, the poet, who died of septicaemia on his way to the Dardanelles. He is buried on the Aegean island of Skyros.
- Vere Harmsworth, son of the newspaper baron Lord Rother-mere, killed at the Battle of the Ancre, November 1916.
- Arthur Asquith, son of the Prime Minister, Herbert Asquith.
- A P Herbert, well-known writer, MP after the war.

During the five years of its existence, the **Royal Naval Division** took part in the defence of Antwerp, 1914; in the Gallipoli Campaign, from the first landings of April 1915, until the final evacuation in January 1916; and fought on the Western Front from May 1916 until the end of the war. It was disbanded in June 1919.

Private John Brough PO/382(s) Royal Marine Light Infantry

- Enlisted in the Royal Marines at York on 17th November 1914.
- With the MEF Dardanelles 23rd May 1915 to 28th July 1915.
- Embarked Folkestone 25th September 1916, Expeditionary Forces, France.
- Taken POW at Passchendaele Ridge, 26th October 1917.
- Remained in captivity in Germany until the Armistice.
- Demobilised 4th March 1919, his 25th birthday, after four years and 108 days' service.

'PO' in his service number indicates that he was assigned to the Portsmouth Division, and 'S' that he was a Short Term recruit, i.e. for the duration of the war.

He left Devonport on 12th May 1915, with the first reinforcements for Gallipoli aboard the troopship *Ivernia*. The first batch of his battalion, the **9th Portsmouth Royal Marine Light Infantry**, had set out for the Dardanelles on 28th–29th February 1915, landing at Anzac Cove on 28th April 1915 in support of the Australians and New Zealanders.

The day after the *Ivernia* sailed, the Marine battalions at Anzac Cove were withdrawn, and the whole of the Royal Naval Division was brought together at Cape Helles on the southern tip of the Gallipoli peninsula. It was here that the troops on the *Ivernia* landed at the end of May 1915, when my father would join his **9th Portsmouth RM Battalion**.

His service in the Dardanelles ended on 28th July 1915, when he was repatriated to England via Glyemenplou Hospital in Alexandria, where the sick and wounded of the Royal Naval Division were taken on evacuation from Gallipoli.

On arrival back in England in early August, he was admitted to the Royal Naval Hospital at Haslar, Southsea, in Hampshire. He was not wounded, so he must have contacted an ailment severe enough for repatriation and nearly six months in hospital. Not until December was he sufficiently recovered to move to a convalescent home. It was the practice to try to locate men as near as possible to where they lived, so John found himself in the familiar surroundings of Whitby, at a convalescent home on Shrub Hill. Here he spent Christmas 1915, visiting his folks at Wethead – the last time, as it turned out, that he would be with his parents, as they both died in 1917 whilst he was in France serving on the Western Front.

On 12th January 1916 he rejoined the **2nd (Portsmouth) RM Battalion** at their Blandford depot in Devon where he remained until embarking at Folkestone for France on 25th September 1916.

From then onwards, he served with the **2nd (Portsmouth) RM Battalion** on the Western Front. He had a spell of home leave in the following September, as the notebook in which he kept his diary as a POW is endorsed 'A present from Tom, Sept 26, 1917, while on leave to England'. This leave might have been on compassionate grounds, as his mother had died. She was buried at Newton-upon-Rawcliffe on 13th September 1917.

Apart from this period of leave, I do not know of any other time when he would be away from his battalion. He would, therefore, take part in the three big battles involving the Royal Naval Division during this period: Battle of the Ancre, November 1916; Battle of Gavrelle, April 1917; First Battle of Passchendaele, October 1917.

The following accounts of the voyage of HMT *Ivernia* give a good idea of my father's likely experiences.

5

Voyage to Gallipoli Aboard HMT Ivernia

Recollections of Thomas Macmillan, Benbow Battalion,
and Reginald Gale, RND Engineers

It was still dark when they marched off to Blanford, where they were greeted by cheering crowds who gave them a rousing send-off. They travelled by train to Devonport.

When the train stopped at Exeter, every man received a paper bag containing bread and cheese, an apple, an orange, and two packets of Woodbines, a gift from the Lady Mayoress and her Ladies' Committee.

On arrival at Devonport, there was only a small group of dock-workers to watch the troops embark. Policemen at each gangway prevented anyone leaving the ship once aboard.

From leaving England until nearing Gibraltar, the weather was very bad. Many of the men suffered ill-effects from the inoculations given prior to departure. The main saloon had to be converted into a temporary hospital, and the ship's doctor called for volunteers to assist. Men were brought in with swollen arms, thoroughly ill, their condition aggravated by sea-sickness. The troop-decks, down in the hold of the ship, had row upon row of bunks, all crowded together with little free space.

After three days at sea, the storm abated. Just after noon, Sunday 16th May 1915, the *Ivernia* dropped anchor off Gibraltar. No one was allowed ashore, but sacks were provided for mail. It is unlikely that these were taken off, as the stay was brief. At 5 p.m., the *Ivernia* sailed into the Mediterranean. After two days at Valetta, Malta, for coaling, the *Ivernia* began the final stage of its voyage.

On the second Sunday at sea, Thomas MacMillan records that a service was held on deck. The sun was gloriously bright, not a ripple on the sea. 'With heads bowed we repeated the Lord's Prayer; it was very moving.'

They then had a pay parade. The money was welcome but what to spend it on? Thomas MacMillan complained that in the ship's little shop, only tinned milk and penny cakes of chocolate, which were now selling for tuppence, remained. The Nestle milk had all gone, and only an inferior brand, selling at the same price, was available. They bought tinned milk and so forth because the food had steadily deteriorated until it was little better than cattle food. Finally, the discontent of the men came to the attention of their officers, and the chief steward was ordered to disgorge some of the food he had hidden away in the hold of the ship.

When the ship reached the Greek archipelago, everyone came on deck to admire the beautiful spectacle of island after island stretching to the horizon. At this point precautions had to be tightened as enemy submarines were reported to be active in the vicinity. This did not disturb the sing-songs on the lower decks, though it brought the war home to them again

At the end of 12 days' sailing, the *Ivernia* drew up outside the boom protecting the entrance to Mudros harbour, on the island of Lemnos. After being detained for hours in a pitch black night, the boom was raised and the *Ivernia* came to rest well within the harbour. Here they remained for several days, and were able to go ashore and to swim in the warm sea; marvellous after the confinement aboard ship. In the village, the shops did a brisk trade in picture postcards.

Transports conveying the remainder of the Brigade duly arrived, together with some smaller ships of the cargo class. One of these, HMS *Hythe*, moored alongside the *Ivernia* and the men transferred across. There was an amazing assembly of warships in the harbour. 'As we sailed past them,' records Thomas MacMillan 'cheering crews lined the decks, and their bands played "Rule Britannia". We all sang and cheered until we had cleared the boom.'

On HMS *Hythe* the deck space was so restricted that the men had to remain standing. The sun had risen by the time they reached the peninsula. 'We were grateful, as the night had been cold,' says Thomas MacMillan.

Drawing close to the barges which had been used in the initial landing, the *Hythe* dropped anchor. The men used the barges as a gangway to land on 'V' Beach, next to the beached SS *River Clyde*. Nearby, the upturned bottom of a British warship loomed out of the sea, looking for all the world like a sea monster asleep.

Reginald Gale recalls that, on landing, an officer welcomed them with the words, 'You are on the Gallipoli peninsula and within a few miles of the trenches. Once you get off this beach you will be visible to the Turks. Do not stand about in groups, nor light fires too close together. It has cost a lot of money to get you out here, and we don't want you killed too soon.'[2]

---

[2] Sellers, L., *RND.*

6

The Gallipoli Campaign

The campaign in Gallipoli was a failure. It ended with the Allies withdrawing their armies in January 1916. Ironically, the evacuation was a great success: there was not a single casualty.

Why the Allies were defeated is not really of concern in following my father's war service, though the incompetence of the generals in charge − one of the reasons for failure − also caused much needless loss of life and suffering of the men in the trenches.

During my father's stay on Cape Helles, Major-General Sir Aylmer Hunter-Weston was in command. John Laffin, in *Damn the Dardanelles*, refers to him as 'The Butcher of Helles'.

Hunter-Weston's aversion to attacking at dusk, during the night and before dawn was a cause of many needless caualties. Always, he had his troops attack in broad daylight. They would charge, spread out in line, against an enemy well dug in, ready and waiting to repel such attacks.

The war correspondent Ashmead-Bartlett stated that Hunter-Weston's excessive optimism 'showed a lamentable ignorance of what it is possible for infantry to achieve in modern warfare'. He realised there was 'something very wrong' with Hunter-Wilson after their first conversation.

Colonel Leslie Wilson, commander of the Hawke Battalion of the **Royal Naval Division**, related an episode concerning an enemy trench in front of his battalion. It was of no importance, but he was ordered to take it. He pointed out that, even if captured, it could not be held. He repeated his protests, but was told the order was to be obeyed. The trench was taken and then, as he had foreseen, his force was bombed out with the loss of three officers and 80 men. Finally, he retired with only six survivors. A Marine battalion was then ordered to retake the trench, which they did, only for them in turn to be driven out, with more unnecessary casualties.

Padre Creighton, who witnessed the 88th Brigade's assault of 28th June, wrote, 'Only about 1300 of the Brigade came back. Some 1700 men lost; practically nothing gained. These things seem to happen every battle. The number of lives simply thrown away unnecessarily is appalling.'

The 156th Scottish Brigade, in its first action, lost 1353 men – nearly half its total strength. Hunter-Weston observed that he was glad of the opportunity of 'blooding the pups'. Such was the man in whose hands rested the fate of so many, including the men of the **Royal Naval Division**.

Cape Helles – The Achi Baba Front

Men and supplies for Cape Helles usually came ashore at the '*River Clyde*' landing place on 'V' Beach. The *River Clyde* was a converted collier, used as a sort of Trojan Horse in the landings of April 1915. It was run aground on 'V' Beach for the troops crammed inside to burst out and secure the beach-head. Unfortunately, little went to plan, and most of the troops were killed by machine gun and rifle fire from the Turks in the surrounding cliffs, many of them not even making the shore.

Eventually, in the weeks that followed, the bridge-head was secured and then pushed a few miles inland, allowing men and supplies to be landed in greater safety.

The *River Clyde* remained firmly beached, forming part of a landing pier. It was, therefore, a familiar sight to all who served at Cape Helles. Although the *River Clyde* was shelled hundreds of times, after the war she was towed off the beach at Sedd-el-Bahr and taken to Malta. Here, engineers patched up her broken plates.

She was renamed *Angela*. Later, after being bought by a Spanish shipping firm, she was again renamed, becoming the *Muraja Y Aurora*. She plied the Mediterranean freight routes for many years until being retired in 1966. The Spanish owners offered her to the British Ministry of Defence, who showed little interest, so the ship was scrapped.

Conditions on Cape Helles

The Allied forces on Cape Helles were confined to a few square miles of territory which they failed, throughout the campaign, to extend by any significant amount. The Turks remained firmly established upon the heights of Achi Baba with their big guns. Nowhere was free from shelling, more so when the Turks set up their guns on the Asia side of the Dardanelles. There was no escape from the deafening din of these guns or the terror of shells crashing from the sky.

Unlike the Western Front, there were no safe areas to which the men could be withdrawn when relieved of front line duty. They took a fatalistic attitude and swam in the sea off Cape Helles despite the shells to enjoy bathing naked, shorn of their dirt encrusted uniforms. I think that an incident involving my father, one of the few he recounted, relates to his time on Gallipoli and to one of these rest areas. There is, perhaps, a moral to it. A companion put much time and effort into constructing an elaborate dug-out, whereas my father nearby merely scraped out a shallow hollow in the earth. A shell landed on his companion, killing him, whilst my father survived unhurt.

The physical conditions on the peninsular were severe so that the British troops lived in utter squalor. Remoteness of Gallipoli from the main British bases meant it was difficult to supply them with even the basic necessities of life. Everything had to be unloaded from small boats onto the makeshift piers on the beach at Cape Hellas open to shellfire from the Turks on Achi Baba. The stores were taken up to the line by mule transport, a dangerous task as Turkish gunners knew where the supply routes were.

It was difficult to set up a cookhouse near enough to the troops on the front line to provide them with hot meals. So usually their rations were bully beef – which melted in its tins in the summer heat – biscuits, bread, jam – often the much hated apricot – cheese, tea and butter. The Huntley and Palmer biscuits were so hard men broke their teeth on them. 'We had tins of jam, always apricot, until we were sick and tired of the thing. We used to use the unopened tins to make doorsteps into the trench' (Cpl Arthur Helmsley).[3]

Throughout the campaign the supply of water was a problem. Whereas the Turks on Achi Baba had plenty of good drinking water, the few wells at Cape Hellas were inadequate. Local supplies captured earlier from the Turks held the high risk of poisoning or pollution. Purifying tablets were issued, all water was supposed to be first chlorinated. To supplement local sources, water was shipped in from Egypt, filled into newly-made kerosene tins and transported by mules to the troops in the trenches.

With all these difficulties, there was little water for washing, although the men were expected to shave, but a little cold water and a blunt razor did little to encourage this. Unable to keep clean, lice became a problem. Many methods were tried to get rid of them, mostly ineffective. Relatives sent tins of anti-lice ointment, Keatings flea powder; camphor in small bags with tape attachment for suspension round the neck was issued until lice were found inside one of these bags.

Men found that if they draped their shirts over one of the many anthills that abounded, the ants would eat the lice. The problem then was to rid their shirts of ants.

Far worse, however, were the vast swarms of flies that were omnipresent. 'The whole side of the trench used to be one black swarming mass. Anything you opened, tin of bully, it would be

---

[3] Steel, N. and Hart, P., *Defeat at Gallipoli*, Papermac, 1995, p. 303.

swarming with flies. If you were lucky enough to have a tin of jam and opened it flies swarmed in. Immediately if you bared any part of your body, you were smothered ...' (Private Harold Broughton).[4]

Fly bags to put over the head were tried into which the wearer put his biscuit and jam then closed up the bottom. He would then eat with buzzing all around, unable to see through the bag for the flies outside.

But the most harrowing of all was the sight and stench of unburied bodies. There could be no formal burial of those who died on the battlefield. The area of ground which made up the front was small in size and was fought over continuously throughout the campaign. Corpses had to be buried in situ. No-man's land was ridiculously narrow and usually under constant and deadly observation. Men killed there could not be recovered until one side or the other advanced, which meant that their bodies could lie unburied for months.

Approaching the peninsular, there was a ghastly smell of corruption. Once ashore and moving inland, it got worse. Private Harry Baker, newly arrived on Cape Helles, records: 'There was a terrible smell in the air and I asked "What's that awful smell?" That's the dead lying beyond our front line two miles away I was told.'[5]

Latrines were primitive a trench six foot deep one yard wide, roughly ten foot long. The seating an arrangement of poles forming an X. Or simply a hole in the ground. No toilet paper (Private Harry Baker).[6]

The combination of unsuitable diet, flies, putrid corpses and inadequate latrines resulted in dysentery affecting almost everyone on Gallipoli ... thousands of men suffered agonies as they lived with a hole in the ground as a toilet, no paper and no means

---

[4] Steel, N. and Hart, P., *Defeat at Gallipoli*, Papermac, 1995, p. 312.
[5] Ibid., p. 354.
[6] Ibid., p. 315.

of cleansing themselves. Dysentery was an awful disease that could rob a man of all vestiges of dignity before it killed him.[7]

Various attempts were made to lessen the problem of how to deal with corpses; one was to spray a solution known as 'Liquid C' onto them, using a hose. It was found to reduce the stench, and to shrink the corpses. (An account of the use of 'Liquid C' is given further on.)

Men tried to cope with these appalling conditions by making light of them. The large gun that fired across the straits was referred to as 'Asiatic Annie', another was called 'Quick Dick'. Trenches were given names from home – Regent Street, Oxford Street, Clapham Junction. Many developed a black sense of humour: 'Just where we entered the trench, which had been built up with dead bodies covered with earth, there was a hand sticking out. It was all dried. One soldier said, "I've known him for a few weeks, he was a dry old stick."[8] We got so callous that, as we passed, we all shook hands with it.'

Another soldier recalled the legs, arms and crown of the head of a body sticking out of the earth at the entrance to a communication trench. The sun had burned all the hair from the head leaving a plain, shiny surface on which someone had written 'RIP' in indelible pencil.

Simple things such as brewing tea in the evening, sharing out a parcel from home, long talks in the starlight of 'when it's all over', were greatly prized. Hours were spent improving their dug-outs, picking lice out of their clothing, cooking their food – pancakes made of flour and water soon became universal – writing letters and diaries.

The men were issued with a green active service envelope on which was printed: 'I certify on my honour that the contents of this envelope refer to nothing but family matters.' This meant the letter

---

[7] Ibid., pp. 315–17.
[8] Steel, N. and Hart, P., *Defeat at Gallipoli*, Papermac, 1995, p. 356.

was censored at base, not at the man's unit. There was also a card for any averse to letter-writing, or unable to do so. It bore the printed words: 'I am quite well' and 'I have been admitted to hospital, sick, wounded' – the sender deleted whichever did not apply

Offensives, June and July 1915

During June and July 1915, the period of my father's service in Gallipoli, the fighting at Cape Helles was the heaviest of the campaign. A series of frontal attacks were launched against the Turks. These were all of short duration – a day or two or even less. All followed the same pattern of trench warfare: a preliminary artillery bombardment, a charge by the infantry, counter-attack by the enemy and, finally, a confused struggle to secure the line.

Nowhere, at any time, were any important objectives gained. At the end of it all, the Allies were hardly any closer to Achi Baba, and the Turks were no nearer to driving the Allies into the sea. Even in the killing of men, neither side could claim the advantage. Total casualties were about the same for each: some 57,000 men.

7

Extracts from the War Diary of the Royal Marine Brigade
RND *Issue 23*

[Luckily for the Royal Marine Battalions they did not take part in the 3rd Battle of Krithia, 4th June, when the **RND** suffered very heavy losses. The action of 23rd June involved only one company of the Portsmouth Battalion, so I do not know if my father took part. He was, of course, present in the actions of 12th–14th July.]

1915

30th May
In bivouac. Reinforcements of 4 Captains, 7 Lieutenants, 9 Sergeants, 8 Corporals and 472 Privates [one of them was my father] arrived.

1st–3rd June
Fatigues by day and night.

4th June
RM Brigade in general reserve for advance which took place on this day. No movement of the Brigade took place.
[The Collingwood Battalion, which came out with my father on the *Ivernia*, suffered so heavily that it had to be disbanded and the few survivors allocated to other battalions.]

7th June
PM Brigade ordered to relieve 1st RN Brigade in the RND front line. Relief carried out during the afternoon and completed by 10.15 p.m. as follows – Right Sector, Deal Battalion; Centre Sector, **Portsmouth Battalion**; Left Sector, Plymouth Battalion; 2nd line, Benbow Battalion.

9th June
Turks active at head of Gully dividing Centre and Left Sectors of our line. Various steps were taken to counteract this activity, but the speed with which the enemy carried out their digging operations enabled them to establish a series of trenches penetrating far down the Gully to within a short distance of our line.

11th June
An artillery bombardment of these works was tried during the afternoon but was of little use owing to the proximity of our own trenches. The Plymouth Battalion completed a 2nd communication trench from the head of the Mule Track to the Diagonal which it occupied.

Night of 11th–12th June
The **Portsmouth Battalion** dug a new fire trench about 30 yards in length between two sap heads with a view to enfilading the enemy works in the Nullah. Two men were killed and three wounded in this operation.

[A sap is a short trench dug towards the enemy line; enfilade is gunfire that rakes a position from end to end; a Nullah is a gully or watercourse, often dried up.

An activity of trench warfare in Gallipoli, very much akin to mediaeval sieges, was mining. A tunnel would be dug under the trench parapet into no-man's land, from which point a sap would be continued towards the enemy lines. Some of the earth would be bagged, the rest thrown over the sides to heighten the trench walls.

The end of the sap would then be barricaded with the bags of earth, forming a new bombing post nearer to the enemy.

All along the front line, these saps were dug. Eventually, the infantry would dig trenches from one sap to next. Though dangerous work, it advanced the front line without the necessity of 'going over the top'. As the Turks did the same, the opposing front lines often became close together. Efforts were even made to tunnel beneath enemy trenches and blow them up, much as the sappers of old did.]

Thirty men of the Royal Scots and the Warwickshire Regiment were buried by the Chatham Battalion, and seven cartloads of arms, ammunition and equipment were collected and returned to Ordnance Store.

12th June
P.M. The Chatham Battalion relieved the **Portsmouth Battalion** in the Centre Sector, the latter going into reserve at the Brown House and Backhouse Post. The Plymouth Battalion in the Left Sector extended its front as far as the Small Nullah.

13th June
Work on various saps and general improvement and upkeep of trenches was in progress.

14th June
The **RM Brigade** was relieved in the trenches by the 1st RN Brigade, relief completed by 8 p.m.

21st June
Very heavy French bombardment of Turkish lines opposite them, followed by an attack. Some trenches taken. **RM Brigade** was to have relieved 1st RN Brigade but postponed because of French attack.

22nd June
Began relieving 1st RN Brigade in trenches at 10 a.m. Plymouth Battalion in Left Sector, **Portsmouth Battalion** in Centre Sector, Chatham Battalion in Right Sector.

23rd June
Quiet day. 10 p.m. one company of Portsmouth Battalion, Major Grover, advanced and took Turkish trench. Heavily bombed by Turks shortly after. Forced to retire with loss of Major Grover, 2 officers and about 60 men. [Hardly a quiet night.]

24th June
Evening, some enemy shelling round Brigade HQ at Backhouse Post.

10 p.m. advanced the Centre and Right line from Sap No.10 on right to Rectangle E. of Nullah. About 50 yards not quite completed by daylight. Some 30 casualties on left. The enemy trench, taken and lost on 23rd, now continued back to their main fire trench, forming a salient. New work seen opposite E. corner of Rectangle in enemy fire trench. Artillery fire ordered here.

[from Divisional War Diaries: Portsmouth and Chatham Battalions attempted to dig a trench. Chatham Btn were very successful but **Portsmouth Btn** came under a very accurate rifle fire and were forced to retire (11 p.m.) after digging to a depth of from 1 to 2 ft.]

25th June
Quiet day. Enemy was shelled by French with high-explosive.

26th June
Heavy shelling by the enemy of the Plymouth Battalion in Left Sector Sap. Great damage to the trenches; 4 killed, 8 wounded. Evening, some shelling around Brigade HQ.

27th June
Again, considerable shelling of the Left Sector

28th June
Relieved by 1st RN Brigade, returned to bivouac.

4th July
In bivouac. Heavily shelled 5 p.m. to 6 p.m. by field guns. Little damage due to poor quality of the shells. Large explosion of ammunition in the French Sector.

6th July
RND Sector handed over to the Lowland Division, 155th Brigade taking over our trenches.
[For nine weeks, the **RND** had been in the trenches, holding the sector of the line that adjoined the French sector. Both officers and men were suffering from severe mental and physical exhaustion and the ravages of dysentery. The Division was now only a shadow of the fighting force which had originally landed, and it had to be withdrawn from the front for a rest. In July 1915, because of such heavy casualties, the **RND** was reorganised into just two Brigades:

1st (R. Naval) Brigade
Drake Btn, Nelson Btn, Hawke Btn, Hood Btn.

2nd (R. Naval) Brigade
1st Marine Btn Chatham/Deal, **2nd Marine Btn Portsmouth/** Plymouth, Anson Btn, Howe Btn.]

9th July
Four machine guns of RM Brigade mounted near Brigade HQ against hostile aeroplanes. In the evening, Plymouth Battalion sent to trenches at Clapham Junction as reserve battalion to 42nd Division. **Portsmouth Battalion** as standby reserve.

10th July
Plymouth Battalion returned to bivouac at 8.30 a.m. Chatham and **Portsmouth Battalions** on fatigues.

11th July
Fatigues.

12th July
Battle of Achi Baba Nullah
[The information in the RM War Diary for 12th–13th July is long and detailed. So I give it further on. What follows are accounts from other sources.]

8

Battle of Achi Baba Nullah

The objective was to advance the centre sector to bring it into line with the sectors on each flank. It was to be carried out by the Scottish 52nd Division. The **RND**, resting from their earlier ordeals, were supposed to be in support only. However, they had to mount a full-scale assault on the Turkish lines the following day.

Steve Newman (*Gallipoli Then and Now*) says that Lt-General Hunter-Weston, on the day after the initial assault, became concerned about a possible Turkish counter-attack.

He decided to use the worn-out troops of the **Royal Naval Division** to carry out a new attack, timed for 1630 hours. The battalions chosen were the Chatham, Nelson and **Portsmouth**. None was issued with amended trench maps, and no one told them that trench E12 (the supposed Turkish 'third trench') on this part of the front was incomplete and impossible to defend.

To make matters worse, as the communication trenches were so clogged with casualties, it was decided that the men would go over the top from the old British line, exposing them to Turkish fire for far longer than would otherwise have been necessary.

The troops, who did not receive their orders until 1500 hours, were still 20 minutes away from their start line when the short bombardment came to an end. By the time they were in a position to start their attack, the Turks had recovered and were ready and waiting.

On the right, the Chatham Battalion made no headway at all, while the **Portsmouth Battalion**, attacking in the centre, came under heavy shrapnel fire. By the time they reached the most advanced of the British trenches held by the 1/7th Highland Light

Infantry, they had already suffered severe casualties. Still they pushed on and gallantly succeeded in taking E12. However, as was already known, this trench was untenable, and the few survivors were quickly forced to withdraw.

An even bitter blow befell the Nelson Battalion, ordered to take trenches E12a and E12b. Having suffered the same shrapnel ordeal as the **Portsmouth Battalion**, and machine gun fire from the flanks, they reached their objectives. As they leapt into the newly 'captured' trench, believing they had achieved their goal, they found it was already held by men of the 52nd Division. Headquarters had got it seriously wrong.

This advance to capture a position that had already been taken, added to the futile attack by the Chatham and **Portsmouth battalions**, cost some 500 men and 24 officers, including both Royal Marine Light Infantry commanding officers.

Nigel Steel and Peter Hart, in *Defeat at Gallipoli*, record that the objectives of the attack of 12th July − to capture the first three Turkish trenches − caused confusion as, in many areas, no third trench had been completed. The attacking 52nd Division found only a dummy trench, a foot deep, which was impossible to hold. They were forced to draw back to the second of the captured trenches. By dawn, 13th July, they were almost spent. Few were keeping a lookout; many were asleep, totally exhausted.

Hunter-Weston, fearing a major Turkish counter-attack, decided to use his only reserve, the **RND**, although he had himself reported them unfit for offensive action. The **Royal Marine Brigade** was ordered to attack at 16.30 on 13th July in conjunction with the French on their right. In circumstances of dreadful confusion, the orders were late in reaching the battalions, and the Chatham Battalion failed to attack, leaving the **Portsmouth** and Nelson Battalions to attack alone. To make matters worse, they were ordered to start their attack from the original British front line, so having to cross 400 yards of open ground, although communication trenches were, by then, available from which they could have attacked from a point much nearer to the enemy positions. The lines that the survivors of this attack reached were already held by the Scottish 157th Brigade, who were aghast at the manner of the assault. In the Horseshoe trench beside the Achi Baba Nullah, Lt Millar of the 5th Argyll and Sutherland Highlanders greeted them with, 'What the ——— do you want?'

Many of the Marines attempted to push on, but to no avail. The misunderstanding over the non-existent Turkish third trench was replayed, and they were caught in the open. All that was achieved for a loss of over 500 casualties was a modest reinforcement of the front line.

For two days, HQ received no reports from **Portsmouth Battalion**. On 14th July, Drake Battalion finally managed to contact them in a captured Turkish trench. Only one officer of the Portsmouth Battalion was not killed or wounded; the number of men lost was disastrous.

Douglas Jerrold, Adjutant of Hawke Battalion RND, later wrote:

> Only those who actually witnessed it can imagine the unbeliev-
> able confusion of the battle; conditions were well nigh un-
> endurable. Some of the worst scenes ever, on any battlefield of
> WW1, were crowded into these forty-eight hours of continuous
> fighting along the narrow, half-mile front at Achi Baba, where
> many hundreds of men lay dead and dying, where a burning sun
> had turned the bodies of the slain to a premature corruption,
> where there was no resting place free from physical contamin-
> ation, where the air, the surface of the ground, and the soil
> beneath the surface were alike poisonous, foetid, corrupt.[9]

The strain of this battle, and of the earlier offensives, broke the health of the men. By the end of July, not 10 per cent of them would have been considered fit for duty in the quietest sector of the front had they been in France. In Gallipoli, at this time, any who could walk to the trenches were considered fit.

---

[9] Sellers, L., *RND.*

9

War Diary of the Royal Marine Brigade
RND *Issue 23 (continued)*

Battle of Achi Baba Nullah

Trenches had been dug across the peninsula at Cape Helles, from the beaches right up to the most advanced front-line positions. It was possible for a man to walk miles without showing his head above ground.

Sauchiehall Street trench ran parallel to Achi Baba Nullah up to the White House and Brown House positions. Beyond these shack-like buildings, a system of interlaced trenches led forward towards Achi Baba. One main junction was called Piccadilly Circus.]

12th July
Brigade, less Deal Battalion, in Corps Reserve from 0600 hrs.

At 1200 hrs, Chatham Battalion was ordered to Backhouse Post in support of the 52nd Division who were carrying out an attack on the Turkish trenches E10, E11, E12, E13, F12 and F12a.

At 1600 hrs, Plymouth and **Portsmouth Battalions** also ordered to Backhouse Post. Chatham Battalion now to move to the old French lines in the rear of Backhouse Post; thence, in support of our Right Flank, to the continuation of Parsons and Trotman Roads to the east.

155th Brigade having captured the line S.T.P. and the lines in the rear, Plymouth Battalion to support 6th Highland Light Infantry in area west of the Nullah.

Portsmouth Battalion to Trotman Road with left on Oxford Street.

In the evening, 52nd Division had captured all the trenches within F11, F11a, E13a, E12, E11, T, D11, B5. Some doubt as to P.T. as communications held by Turks

13th July

Very difficult to find out the exact line held by the 52nd Division. West of the Nullah, the Plymouth Battalion RMLI, sent in support last night, found themselves in sole occupation of the captured trenches, and which they hold, as the 155th Brigade has withdrawn to Nelson and Plymouth Avenues.

To the east of the Nullah, the 52nd Division suddenly left their trenches and fell back, followed by a few Turks. Plymouth Battalion drove off the enemy, taking 12 prisoners and capturing two machine guns. The **Portsmouth Battalion** situated to the east, and the Plymouth Battalion, on the west bank of the Nullah, got the 52nd back into some of their trenches.

1230 hrs the line held was F11, F11a, F12, F12a, F13 [for 30 yards], E11 [to sap joining E12a to E10a], E.10-A-R-W-Z, and A-Z by 2nd Turkish trench.

Ground lost E13 and rest of E11 and E12.

1400 hrs Chatham, **Portsmouth** and Nelson Battalions under Brigadier General Trotman were ordered to attack and retake T-S-P-E12-E13a at 1630 hrs.

Accordingly, at 1500 hrs, the Brigadier met the commanding officers of these battalions at the junction of Regent Street and Trotman Road.

Chatham Battalion to attack T.S. track west of E. in E11.

Portsmouth Battalion to attack track-2a.

Nelson Battalion to attack 2a-Nullah.

1540 hrs Battalion commanders left the conference.

1600 hrs bombardment by the French guns commenced.

Moving over open ground to present front line by 1615 hrs.

Brigade Order

1. The front T-E11-E12-E13a is to be attacked at 1630 today by the Chatham Battalion on the right, **Portsmouth Battalion** in the centre, Nelson Battalion on the left, from Parsons Road and Trotman Road.

2. Chatham Battalion will attack from point T to the track 100 yards north-west of S, just west of E in E11. **Portsmouth Battalion** from the above track to a point in E12, 150 yards true north of junction between E11 and E12 just north-east of point 2. Nelson Battalion from the above point to Achi Baba Nullah … Plymouth Battalion will continue to hold their present position on north-west side of the Achi Baba Nullah.

3. Battalions will move forward from Parsons and Trotmans Roads at 1615 hrs and will assault by orders of Company Commanders at 1630.

4. The French are attacking on the right of the Chatham Battalion on frontage T-O.12.

5. Battalions will advance in two waves − one man per yard in one wave, one man per two yards in second wave.

6. Consolidating party of about one man per 5 yards will accompany both waves.

7. Special bombing parties will be told off.
Chatham Battalion will deal with O.11-T, S.
Portsmouth Battalion will deal with A-P, 1-2, 3-4.
Nelson battalion will deal with 5, 6, 6a etc.

8. Brigade HQ will be established 50 yards south of junction between Trotman Road and Regent Street.

1630 hrs the attack commenced except by the Chatham Battalion. Enemy pouring in a very heavy shrapnel fire. On our left, Nelson Battalion advanced and took the line E12b, E11 and J. They then advanced further but could not hold this ground.

The **Portsmouth Battalion** occupied E11 from 6 to Telegraph line and E12 but, not being able to dig in on E12 (which is not a trench) when under fire, and not being able to gain touch with Chatham Battalion, they came back to the line E11 to P.

The French on our right, who also advanced, had to fall back as well.

Casualties very heavy. Colonel Eveleigh commanding Nelson Battalion was killed. Nelson Battalion report only 4 officers and 120 men left. However, subsequently, about 280 all told were collected.

Portsmouth Battalion had Colonel Luard killed. All the officers were killed or wounded except temporary Captain Gowney, who was wounded the next day, leaving just the Transport Officer and the Quartermaster as the only officers in the battalion.

14th July

During the night, Drake Battalion sent up to support and, later, relieve the **Portsmouth Battalion**, who returned to Backhouse Post.

All trenches are in a *very* bad state, with rotting bodies in heaps everywhere, and our men are obliged to wear respirators. Even then, vomiting is very bad, and there is much sickness.

15th July

P.M. Highland Light Infantry were withdrawn from the firing line and from E10 position.

The enemy are holding P-S-T and part of P-A.

1930 hrs the Turks reported massing in P-S-T, but no attack resulted.

During the night, the enemy attempted to work on our front, but we opened fire and this work ceased.

16th July

Battalions in sector relieved by 2nd RN Brigade

17th July

Portsmouth Battalion permanent fatigue of 200 men at Backhouse Post. Remainder, fatigues as required.

19th–20th July
Fatigues.

[As my father was evacuated from Gallipoli at the end of July 1915, I have not detailed the campaign any further. The **Royal Naval Division** continued to be involved in the fighting right up to the Allies' withdrawal in January 1916, and were among the last of the units to leave Gallipoli. The 2nd Royal Naval Brigade then went to Salonica in the area of the Gulf of Stavros, whilst the 1st Royal Naval Brigade policed the islands of Tenedos, Imbros and Lemnos.]

10

Notes on Gallipoli

Backhouse Post

At the entrance to Backhouse Post was a sign, fashioned from a biscuit tin into the shape of a triangle, on each side of which was roughly painted in black letters 'Backhouse Post'. It marked a position familiar to every **RND** officer and man on the peninsula, as it was the site of the Brigade HQ of Commodore Oliver Backhouse, Commander of the 2nd Naval Brigade. When the front advanced after the May assaults and the Brigade HQ moved forward, the 'Post' became the Divisional Supply Dump, and was the limiting point for wheeled vehicles. Although not free from enemy observation and shell fire, it had the advantage of some trees for shade and a nullah or stream.

When the 52nd Highland Division replaced the **Royal Naval Division** on this sector of the front, they also used Backhouse Post as their supply dump. It was, therefore, a notable Gallipoli landmark, often referred to in orders, and told of in histories.

The tin sign was recovered and brought back to Britain, where it is now an exhibit in the Regimental Museum of The Royal Scots in Edinburgh Castle.

Sleeping

The men slept in what dug-outs they had managed to hollow out in the side of the trench or, more usually, just on the bottom of the trench:

There is so little room for the men to sleep in the firing line that many of them have to sleep on the firing line step. Some actually prefer to lie full length on the floor, putting up with the kicks of the patrolling officers. They never wake. I suppose a really tired man seldom does. (Lt George Hughes)[10]

Falling asleep:

As an officer, I knew what a serious matter it was to be court martialled for being asleep on sentry duty. Also, it was a serious matter if, as an officer, you caught somebody asleep and did not report it. So what we used to do was to go down the trenches and, if we thought a man was asleep, we'd knock his legs from under him, then go on twenty yards, then turn back and come and talk to him. He was invariably awake by then! (Lt George Horridge)[11]

The sentry, of course, was only too aware of his peril, but exhaustion and ill-health made it a physical impossibility to guarantee not to go to sleep.

I was on watch, and I don't remember anything until I fell with a crash to the bottom of the trench. Rifle and bayonet – it was a wonder I didn't kill myself. But I never thought about being hurt. I scrambled back up as quick as I could because I'd be for a court martial. (O/S Steve Moyle, Drake Btn, RND)[12]

The men helped each other as much as they could, given their own exhaustion:

There were lots of cases where men fell asleep and their pals

---

[10] Steel, N. and Hart, P., *Defeat at Gallipoli*, Papermac, 1995, p. 320.
[11] Ibid., p. 322.
[12] Ibid.

would wake them. I remember lots of times I shut my eyes then, all of a sudden, I was awake; somebody had given me a kick. We were so exhausted. You would stand on the fire step, and you used to slide down the wall onto your backside, at the bottom of the trench. No idea, no warning. (A/B Joe Murray, Hood Btn, RND)[13]

Dress

Conditions made it impossible to maintain any concept of 'spit and polish'. The men's uniforms were usually dirty and ragged. Many wore abbreviated forms with their thick trousers cut down to shorts. Any type of headgear would be worn.

Bombing

The troops on both sides turned to an old weapon, the hand grenade, or bomb as it was then known. Because of the proximity of the opposing front lines, it was an ideal weapon. Initially, the British were not supplied with hand grenades, and the first ones used were improvisations. Any odd pieces − stones, empty cartridges, bits of metal, nails, etcetera − were stuffed into a jam tin, together with an explosive and fuse. The fuse was lit and, after it began to fizz, the bomb held for two or three seconds before being hurled towards the enemy trench.

Bomb-throwing was nerve-racking, and there were many accidents in the trenches: 'It was the easiest thing in the world to hit the parapet, then down the bomb fell on top of you' (A/B Joe Murray, Hood Btn, RND).

Another contrivance from the Middle Ages was also used: a wooden catapult. This would be set up in the rear of the front line

---

13 Ibid.

to hurl bombs onto the Turks. The British troops in between were not impressed:

> The operators were brigade people and, as soon as we heard they were coming, everybody would say, 'Those bastards have come, take cover.' They'd set themselves up and start firing. The bombs would go anywhere – to the right, to the left – you never knew where they were going. Instead of facing the enemy, everybody in the front line would be looking backwards to see that the bombs weren't coming near them. And laugh! When you saw a bomb going right smack in the middle of another company. Laugh! They would rush left and right to get out of the way of this awful bomb. (2nd Lt Eric Wolton)[14]

Artillery Bombardment

A problem for the artillery supporting an infantry attack was to identify the enemy trenches which had been captured. The infantry carried forward screens, khaki towards the enemy, red towards their own guns. These proved unreliable because the Turks often recaptured trenches by counter-attack, and left the screens in position.

Brigadier General William Marshall, from a rear observation point, had noted that the British trenches could be clearly identified by the shimmering rows of ration tins lined up behind them, giving him the idea for the attacking troops to carry a metal disc on their backs.

Henceforth, a metal triangle, cut from tin, with sides about 12 inches long, was strapped to the back of each man in the attacking line.

It proved effective (especially as Major-General Hunter-Weston seldom gave his troops the protection of darkness in which to attack).

---

[14] Ibid., p. 341.

Commander-in-Chief Sir Ian Hamilton, from his observation post much further back, watched an assault on 28th June by the 86th/87th Brigades. He was entranced by the success of the tin triangles:

> The spectacle was extraordinary. From my post I could follow the movements of every man. One moment after 11 a.m., the smoke pall lifted and moved slowly on, with a thousand sparkles of light in its wake, as if someone had quite suddenly flung a big handful of diamonds onto the landscape.[15]

Snipers

Another constant threat to the troops on Gallipoli was the Turkish sniper. From their higher ground, the Turks could train their sights on the British lines. Even after the trench lines were properly established, these snipers remained a mortal threat to the unwary. An unnoticed gap in a trench parapet of a few inches could spell sudden death.

Discipline

From the letters of Sir Archibald Paris, Commanding Officer, **Royal Naval Division**, 1914–1916, written to his childhood friend Mrs Christine Pilkington, *RND* issue 16:

> 30th March, 1916 – [on the island of Mudros on garrison duty] ... even the Naval Division sometimes gets into trouble, witness a row of malefactors outside my window, tied to stakes, doing what is known as Field Punishment No.1, a very unpleasant way

---

[15] Ibid.

of spending a couple of hours when the day's work is done. Quite like the old days of the pillory.[16]

Liquid 'C'

Sanitary Conditions Gallipoli, *RND* issue 5

As it was often impossible to bury the dead of both friend and foe, men in the trenches were living with, or close to, rotting corpses. In the hot summer months of 1915, the stench was awful and the risk of infection great. Experiments were made in spraying human corpses and dead animals with a liquid, referred to as liquid 'C', as a deodorant and insecticide.

The body of a Turk, killed eight days previously and buried five days in the parapet of a trench, was exhumed. Decomposition was in full progress and the stench was terrible, and the carcass covered in flies which were breeding in it. The body was lying on its side. About one gallon of the liquid was squirted from a garden spray. Some of the flies that were on the body were killed immediately and the remainder repelled. The stench abated almost immediately. The corpse was left exposed, as it was not possible to turn it in the daytime because of enemy sniping. Two days later, there was a complete absence of smell, and only a few flies, which settled then rose again. The size of the body had markedly shrunk.

Three or four bodies immediately behind the firing line were sprayed with the fluid. They had been dead for some time and the smell in the trench was very offensive. The smell was damped down entirely by the fluid. In trench warfare, the use of this substance ought to be invaluable.

---

[16] Ibid.

Manure Heaps

A selected area on a large manure heap was sprayed with the fluid. Larvae were swarming in the manure. Those sprayed immediately died. On visiting this again, there had been some recent hatching out of larvae.

The most that can be said is that the flies were repelled and a certain number of larvae killed.

Notes concerning the fluid sent for trial – for human corpses:
We have been much at a loss hitherto as to how to deal with the decomposing corpses lying in front of and round about our firing line, too exposed to be reached day or night by our burial parties, and yet so close that the most disgusting stench blows from them into our trenches. We have tried spraying this fluid from the trenches over the parapet onto the corpses and it has proved very effective as a deodorant, as a fly deterrent and, slightly, as a preservative, allowing the corpse to shrivel up and mummify without foul smelling decomposition.

A few concluding notes on Gallipoli

Lt. Basil Bedsmore, Hawke Battalion, **RND**:

> You must realise that on the peninsula at Helles you were always subject to shell fire; you might get it anywhere. If you were in the reserve camp, which meant living underground in dug outs, you were not able to move about much in the daytime as this would attract fire.

Nearly everyone who survived Cape Helles had their 'near miss' story. I think an incident involving my father, one of the few I remember him recounting, would have occurred at the rest area there. Apparently, a companion had put much time and effort into constructing an elaborate dugout, whereas my father nearby merely scraped out a shallow hollow in the earth. A direct shell hit killed his companion whilst my father survived unharmed.

Finally, another of my father's few recollections, told to my mother, was of charging uphill at the Turks over the bodies of men killed in earlier assaults. This would be on 13th July in the Battle of Achi Baba.

So concludes my father's service in the Dardanelles.

11

France

The second chapter in my father's war service, the Western Front, began in September 1916, when he was drafted to France. **The Royal Naval Division** left the Dardanelles for France, disembarking at Marseilles in May 1916. They moved to an area of pleasant villages north-west of Arras.

In July, the Division came under Army control as the 63rd (RN) Division and was formed into two brigades, plus a third brigade of four Army battalions:

188th Brigade – Howe Btn, Anson Btn, 1st RMLI Btn, 2nd RMLI Btn.

189th Brigade – Hood Btn, Drake Btn, Hawke Btn, Nelson Btn.

190th Brigade – 1st HAC Btn, 4th Bedford Btn, 7th Royal Fusiliers, 10th Dublin Fusiliers.

The first major action involving the **RND** in France was the assault on the German-held salient around Beaumont Hamel in the Battle of the Ancre.

On 4th October, the **RND** took over a section of front line from Serre almost as far as Beaumont Hamel. (By this time, my father would have rejoined the 2nd RM Battalion.)

On 14th October, General Paris, the Divisional Commanding Officer, was severely wounded by a shell. He had a leg amputated and was repatriated.

He was replaced by a newly promoted Army Major General, Cameron Shute, who was difficult to get along with, a stickler for discipline. He disapproved of the Naval Battalions' ways, complaining that 'there are no real sailors among them, yet they receive nearly double Army pay; there are no smart battalions, and the standard of physique and training is below that of the Army'. Naval titles were 'ridiculous' he claimed, and discipline 'lamentable'.

Not surprisingly, he alienated both officers and men, and prompted Lieut A P Herbert to write a ditty, soon turned into a popular song to the tune of 'Tarpaulin Jack' which the **RND** troops sang as they marched:

> The general inspecting the trenches exclaimed with a horrified
>   shout,
> 'I refuse to command a division which leaves its excreta about.'
> But nobody took any notice, no one was prepared to refute,
> That the presence of shit was congenial compared with the
>   presence of Shute.
> And certain responsible critics made haste to reply to his words,
> Observing that his staff advisors consisted entirely of turds.
> For shit may be shot at odd corners and paper supplied there to
>   suit,
> But a shit would be shot without mourners if somebody shot
>   that shit Shute.

A few days later, despite his harsh criticisms, Shute issued orders for the Division, in the forthcoming Battle of the Ancre, to take on one of the strongest defended sectors of the Western Front.

On 2nd November, the whole Division was paraded for his inspection. They stood out in lines for three hours in pouring rain awaiting his arrival, then the inspection was called off. The men went into barns and lit fires in an attempt to dry out. The next day, they paraded again. This time, the General did arrive. He told them:

> The place you are going to attack now is one of the most formid-
> able parts on the whole Western Front. The Germans have been
> there umpteen months, and it's covered with dug-outs. We have

made five different attempts, as you know, but we must get that ridge. If we don't take it, the whole advance on the Somme is in danger. We must have that ridge at all costs. I am going to tell you this much. You know what you have to do.

And he added: 'The more prisoners you take, the less food you will get, because we have to feed them out of your rations.'

12

Battle of the Ancre, 13th–14th November 1916
from RND *Issue 2*

During the four weeks from the middle of September 1916, the men of the **RND** were preparing for their first major action on the Western Front.

From the outset, this operation appeared to be ill-starred. The popular commanding officer of the **RND**, Sir Archibald Paris, had been seriously wounded on 14th October and replaced by an army officer, Major General C. D. Shute, who regarded the Naval Division as lacking army discipline and efficiency and had resolved to 'shake them up'. The attention of the officers in the four weeks prior to the attack was taken up with changes of routine, standards of dress, mounting of guards etc.

In addition, the weather was appalling. Rain fell practically unceasingly, and it was cold. Besides an almost total lack of protective dug-outs, the communication trenches were under enemy fire. The front line was constantly flooded with freezing mud, and there was little space for resting, sheltering, or even moving about.

Whilst awaiting the final preparations for the battle, the **RND** were either in the line, with all its dangers and discomforts, or engaged in fatiguing work-parties, particularly the digging of extra trenches in which to assemble the troops ready for the attack.

As if all this was not enough, the operation was repeatedly deferred because of bad weather and supply problems behind the lines. By 10th November, when final orders for the attack were issued, most of the **RND** battalions were physically very tired and down to an average strength of 500 (from 700), though morale remained high.

The **RND** occupied a 1200-yard sector immediately north of the Ancre, running at right-angles to the course of what had been a stream but which was now a muddy morass. 189th Brigade were on the right, 188th Brigade on the left, each with a frontage of about 600 yards.

The Division's objectives were four in number:

1. The first wave of four Battalions – right to left, Hood, Hawke, Howe and 1st RMLI – would attack the third line of the German front line trench system – the Dotted Green Line – on the crest of the first ridge, and then consolidate.
2. Following behind, the second wave of four Battalions – right to left, Drake, Nelson, Anson and **2nd RMLI** – would pass through and take the second objective – the Green Line. This was a strongly fortified line along a second ridge about 500 yards beyond Station Road, which ran (and still does) from Beaumont Hamel to a railway halt about 700 yards south of Beaucort village.
3. The Battalions of the first wave would then pass through the Green Line and attack the third objective, Beaucort Trench – the Yellow Line – a further line of trenches south of Beaucort.
4. The second wave of troops, in turn, would pass through the Yellow Line and attack the fourth objective – the Red Line – which was the other side of Beaucort, and then dig in.

For several days leading up to 13th November, about 30 minutes before dawn, a heavy bombardment of the German trenches took place. In the attack, a 'creeping' artillery barrage was to be used – the troops would follow close behind the barrage as it progressed to successive lines of the enemy trenches, a technique that had taken much training and bitter experience to implement.

The original orders also allowed for the assistance of 6 tanks and the use of gas on 'Y' day (the day before the attack) 'if the wind is favourable'.

Movement of the assault troops into the assembly areas began at 1800 hours on 12th November, almost 12 hours before zero hour. The whole Division was involved and so the troops could not all be accommodated in the assembly trenches; many of the first waves had to lie out in the open in no man's land. It was still cold, though warmer than the previous nights. The whole operation was conducted in silence – any warning of an attack being mounted would have brought down enemy fire, which would have been disastrous for the packed lines of **RND**.

The men passed a miserable night in their greatcoats, knowing that the assault, postponed several times before, was now going ahead. It remained dry for the rest of the night but, as dawn approached, a thickening mist began to develop. At zero hour, 5.45 a.m. 13th November, the whole of the battlefield was covered by a very dense fog which persisted for another four or five hours.

The officers synchronised their watches around 4 a.m. and the men were roused at 4.30 a.m. The men of all battalions rolled up their greatcoats and made their final preparations. The artillery had kept up its firing during the night so as not to arouse the enemy's suspicions. At zero hour – exactly 5.45 a.m. – the intense barrage opened up as it had for several days previously. The leading battalions immediately stood up and marched into the gloom, rifles at the port, keeping as close to the creeping barrage as they dared. Visibility was about 50 yards, and it was still dark. Within seven minutes, the whole of the two Brigades had disappeared from the sight of the those few remaining in the British front line.

The 1st and **2nd RMLI** Btns met with disaster from the outset. They were on the left of the Divisional front where the enemy artillery was far more active and hostile, and where there was persistent and accurate fire from machine guns sited in the Beaumont Hamel area. Heavy casualties were suffered, over 50 per cent of them in no-man's land. All four Company Commanders of the 1st RMLI were killed before the battalion crossed the German front line.

Those Marines who escaped the initial slaughter fell behind

and lost the cover of the creeping barrage. Some **2nd RMLI** men managed to pass through 1st RMLI, as planned, and to attack their first objective, Station Road. It was in a shallow hollow, where they were especially vulnerable. They engaged in hand-to-hand fighting, then managed to join up with the remnants of other **RND** Battalions to take part in the successful assault of Beaucort village on the following day. (The OCs of both Marine Battalions won the DSO for gallantry.)

In the centre and left sectors, many casualties were inflicted upon the attacking troops by a German strong-point that had survived both the initial artillery barrage and the creeping barrage. It had to be by-passed and left to be dealt with later. General Shute called for the six tanks allocated in the original plan but, unfortunately, these had been withdrawn. In the event, only three returned, not arriving until after dark. The following morning, one of these tanks managed to approach within point-blank range of the strongpoint, and the garrison of over 400 surrendered. The position consisted of three concrete machine gun posts set in a maze of chalk tunnels, some of which had been constructed in the wars of the the 16th and 17th centuries. The German machine guns down in the dug-out were on lifts raised manually by a winding handle. By being lifted with the crews in position, they were ready for immediate action.

Meanwhile, the 188th Brigade had fought for the rest of the first day and night to establish themselves in the uncaptured German positions.

By late afternoon of 14th November, it was clear that the battalions of the initial assault were exhausted – they had been in close action and under heavy fire for 36 hours. They were to be relieved, but replacements were slow to arrive – not until just after midnight did the new battalions reach the battle zone. By 3 a.m., on the morning of the 15th, 188th and 189th Brigades retired to the old German line prior to marching to Engelbelmer over 5 miles away.

The Battle of the Ancre was a victory. The Germans had been

evicted from immensely strong positions. On the flanks of the **RND**, the other divisions had also done well. Three fortified villages — Beaumont Hamel, Beaucourt and St Pierre Divion — were captured and over 6300 prisoners taken.

The **RND**, however, had paid a terrible price for its achievements. Of 189th Brigade, only 15 officers were unwounded, less than 600 other ranks marched back to Engelbelmer. Although all four Battalion Commanding Officers of the 188th Brigade survived to lead their men out of the battle zone, the average strength of each battalion was 140 — it was 500 when they set out.

So they arrived back in billets much depleted in numbers but confident that they had 'shown Shute what they were made of'. Despite this, Shute wrote again to II Corps that 'gallantry of the **RND** on the Ancre only emphasises the need to reorganise'.

This stopped in January 1917, when it is recorded that 'The zeal of the reformers suddenly abated'. Shute had been told to relax a little.

13

Other Accounts of the Battle of the Ancre
from Trench and Turret *by S. M. Holloway*

Having been put through training and a tour of duty in a fairly quiet sector, the **RND** arrived in the back areas of the Somme battlefield in October 1916, ready to be used in a major assault. This took place on 13th November as the winter rain and mud effectively put an end to the Somme Battle.

The extreme left of the British front line was situated on the River Ancre rather than the River Somme itself, and has the official title of the Battle of the Ancre. In the wider context it was the final chapter in the Battle of the Somme, 1916.

Sgt Meatyard, **2nd Btn RMLI**, recorded:

About 3 a.m. on the morning of the 13th, certain platoons crawled out in no-man's land and got close up to the Germans' barbed wire − there lying flat and still, patiently waiting for zero. At 5.45 a.m., we were ready and waiting, the morning light just beginning to show itself. 2nd RMLI were to advance 15 minutes after the first battalions. At five minutes to six, the CO announced five minutes to go. What a time it seemed going. There was not a sound to be heard. The question − did Fritz know? It was nothing new for him to get wind of an attack and of the time it was coming off, but this time he was apparently taken by surprise. Each morning, at dawn, for the last few days, our guns had been giving him pepper, but no infantry attack took place. I expect he got fed up with these false alarms.[17]

---

[17] Holloway, S. M., *Trench and Turret*, The Royal Marines Museum, Southsea.

Capt. Montagu, Hood Btn: 'It was a weird sight seeing the dim figures of the men advancing in waves through the mist with little bursts of flame coming among them and lighting up the fixed bayonets.'

The RND was suffering heavy casualties. Half the casualties of the two RMLI Battalions occurred before they reached the first German line, over the muddy, shell-pocked slope. Most of these were caused by German heavy machine-gun fire. Before the Dotted Green Line objective had been reached, all the Company Commanders in the 1st Btn RMLI had been killed.

Drake Btn on the extreme right lost heavily in the barrage, their CO was one of those killed.

Hawke and Howe Btns came up against an enemy strongpoint the artillery barrage had missed. Small parties of Hawke Btn reached the Dotted Green Line, their CO wounded.

The Nelson Btn came against the same withering German fire. Many of them fell around the enemy position including their CO. The survivors struggled on to the Dotted Green Line.

Parties of the Anson Btn, also without their CO got to the Green Line.

There was a lot of confusion, which was not surprising. Without the benefit of present day means of communication, messages had to be passed by written note or telephone.

Each Company had 'runners'* but their chance of getting the message through was limited. The more desperate the situation the more likely the 'runner' was to be killed or wounded on his journey. Signallers had to advance under enemy fire, unrolling great rolls of telephone wire as they went. Even if they managed to keep up unhurt, the chances were that shell fire would break the wire.

[* I remember my father saying that he was a 'runner', though when and where I do not know. It could have been here in the Battle of the Ancre, or in the Battle of Gavrelle, or in both, possibly.]

At 7.30 a.m. the advance to the Yellow Line was timed to begin and a barrage commenced. Hood Btn and the remnants of the Drake Btn reached their part of that line without much difficulty, and parties of the Anson Btn and details from 1st and **2nd Btns RMLI** also got there. Meanwhile, the rest of **2nd Btn RMLI** were still on the way to the Station Road:

> The CO, waving his cap above his head, said 'Come on Royal Marines' and over they went to the next trench ... Having passed a stick through the centre hole of the reel (of telegraph wire), I ran forward and the reel unwound as I went along. At about every 15 yards I dropped into a shell-hole and took a breather, then I got my legs free from the mud and made another dash and so on. By this means, I escaped all their bullets and got to my objective. Sgt Meatyard **2nd Btn RMLI**.[18]

Lt-Commander Bernard Freyburg, Hood Battalion, RND:

> At 5.40 a.m., all the assaulting troops fixed their bayonets; they muffled the bayonet catch and ring, and the rifle muzzle, with their greatcoats to deaden the metallic click as the two engaged. Everything was now ready, save the opening and closing of the bolt as they stood up, transferring a cartridge from the magazine to the chamber.
>
> At 5.45 a.m. to the second, the whole sky in the rear was suddenly lit up by hundreds of flashes; the guns had fired. The sound reached us some seconds later and, about seven seconds after the sound, thousands of shells passed a few feet over our heads and burst 150 yards beyond. Our 12 waves were now running hard to get clear of the enemy counter-barrage. Some of our guns were shooting short of the barrage into our assembled troops. They seemed to be dropping very short on our right.
>
> Everywhere was confusion. We were nearly choked by the acrid smell of cordite. In the luminous mist, all we could see were

---

[18] Ibid., p. 56.

lines of phantom figures moving forward with their bodies bent at the middle, rigidly holding their rifles at the high port.[19]

A/B Thomas MacMillan, 188th Brigade Clerk:

The first objective was the enemy's front line system of triple trenches. The second was a road that led to Beaucourt station and which had trenches on each side of it. The third was the trenches which fringed the village of Beaucourt, and the fourth was the village itself which lay on the north side of the river.

The advance of the battalions of the 189th Brigade on the extreme right was comparatively rapid as they enjoyed fairly good cover from enfilade fire. A more difficult task confronted the centre of our advance, which consisted of the left half of 189th Brigade and the right half of **188th Brigade**. In their track was a formidable German redoubt bristling with machine guns which held up the centre and inflicted heavy casualties. The left of our advance out-flanked this strongpoint and reached Station Road. At this stage of the battle, our Division formed a deep curve with its right wing well forward, its centre held up, and its left wing almost as forward as its right. The redoubt held out but our troops who had worked round the flanks joined forces on Station Road and isolated it, leaving its ultimate capture until later.

The German second line was in our possession with the right of their third line as well. At about 8 a.m. next day, the assault of the village was carried out successfully by Hood Battalion led by commander Freyburg.

One of our tanks forced the German machine gun post to surrender.

Our Division had gained all its objectives.[20]

---

[19] Sellers, L., *RND*.
[20] Ibid.

The winter of 1916/17 was one of the coldest on record; the ground had been frozen continuously since mid-December. In these conditions, it was decided to renew the attacks.

Miraumont, 17th February 1917

The **RND** moved into the line around Grandcourt at the end of January 1917, with preparation for offensive action towards Miraumont. The plan was to take the sunken lane opposite Baillescourt Farm. 188 Brigade was allotted the task of taking this line. 2 RM was to provide consolidation parties and form a flank guard on the left flank.

Conditions were generally bad. The ground had been frozen but was now thawing out, leaving the battlefield muddy. There were no trenches as such − they had been blown away − at best there was a line of shell holes. The result was that there were no landmarks, making it difficult to orientate units. Carrying parties and people attempting to get to the front line were disorientated and frequently lost.

Zero hour was 5.45 a.m. and the attack started with terrific artillery support. By 7.15 a.m., Howe Btn had taken their portion of the sunken lane, 1 RM had also taken their part and had pushed out twenty yards beyond to form strongpoints. 2 RM had secured the left flank By 7.30 a.m., the whole objective had been taken.

The following day, at 7.30 a.m., the Germans put down a heavy bombardment on the sunken lane. This was not followed up with an assault as the visibility was poor due to mist. At 10.30 a.m., the mist lifted revealing that a German counter-attack of about two battalions strength was only approximately 300 yards away. Fortunately, at this moment, the line back to HQ was repaired, and an SOS message was sent. Within two minutes, a barrage fell on the Germans and they turned and ran, their counter-attack crushed.

That was the last attempt to retake the ground.

188 Brigade units were relieved on 19th February. The starting

strength of 1 RM was around 500, at the end only 100 were fit for duty. Seven officers and 71 men were killed, some 300 wounded. These casualties were virtually all caused by the bombardment whilst waiting to attack, few were killed in the assault itself. Howe Battalion lost 2 officers and 20 men killed, with around 200 wounded. 2 RM had 1 officer and 5 men killed.

14

Conditions in Early 1917 as Described by
Lt Commander Bernard Freyberg, Hood Battalion[21]

[Although this account relates to the Hood Battalion, the experiences described would be common to the rest of the **RND**, including my father's **2nd RM Battalion**.]

Some of the worst weather conditions of the war were experienced in February and March of 1917. These adverse times were acutely felt on the Somme owing to the enemy's policy of razing to the ground – before withdrawing – all the buildings and trees that our shelling had not already levelled. Whilst the Germans retired to prepared positions, our troops occupied the old trench system. In winter time, this was a morass of mud and desolation, miles across, with only the belts of barbed wire entanglements, mostly of German origin, projecting above the earth's crust. The sole remaining link with the rest of our army was a single-way, congested, plank road, which had been built forward, plank by plank, across the mud before the hard frosts had set in.

During the hard frosts, the ground became like iron; no impression could be made upon it even with a pick, so the men were forced to take cover in shell-holes. The petrol tins of drinking water froze hard and had to be opened with a tin-opener, then pieces of ice chipped off with a bayonet and forced into water-bottles, where they remained frozen until mealtimes. If a man wanted a drink, he

---

[21] Sellers, L., *RND*.

had to thaw the ice by placing the water-bottle inside his shirt. Washing and shaving was impossible.

The occupied shell-holes were usually half-full of ice, upon which the men had to kneel or lie during the day; at night only, was it possible to move about and stretch out the creases that had been frozen into their bodies during the cramped hours of daylight. Men were often frozen to death as they lay facing the enemy, their rifles still tightly gripped as if ready for use. Inspecting officers sometimes arrested what they believed were sleeping sentries, only to discover their melancholy error. Under these conditions of cold, our wounded stood little or no chance; drowsiness followed any loss of blood which, in turn, gave way to death. Even without the harassment we received from the enemy, our Higher Command never allowed us to rest for an hour without ordering us to attack, to raid or to reconnoitre.

Under such conditions, men were never kept in the line for more than 48 hours. They marched in with two days' rations of food and water, wearing leather jerkins and sheepskin gloves, and carrying blankets to wrap around their legs, and sandbags and waterproof sheets to sit on. Greatcoats were generally left at transport lines to ensure having at least one dry article of clothing to sleep in on returning to rest.

During periods out of the line, the infantry remade the road and railway between Thiepval and Grandcourt, vital for conveying supplies, but the enemy could demolish them again far more quickly than we could rebuild, so we were constantly short of the necessities for comfort.

Our sufferings, however, were nothing compared with those of the horses standing in the open with no cover at all. They had been clipped to prevent 'scab' – which was prevalent – and their hay and oats had been cut below a working ration because of shortages. It was heart-breaking to see them huddled together for protection. Horses died in large numbers, usually dropping from exhaustion, and their carcasses and skeletons littered both sides of the road.

When the Royal Naval Division was exhausted by the active

operations of February and the first week of March, we came back permanently to our camp on the side of a hill just clear of enemy observation. There was no shelter from the cutting north wind, and we were all in a debilitated state, suffering from loss of sleep owing to the cold, which was often 30° below zero. The wind took the skin from our faces and hands, while our ears were covered with frost-bite sores. Men spent six hours working and two hours marching between camp and work. There were no games or social side to our lives, and we never saw a civilian from one week to another; consequently, our minds were always focused on the war.

On 10th March, the rumour came that a large attack to the north was imminent (The Battle of Gavrelle). On 18th March, working parties were cancelled and, on the following day, we marched out of camp, heading northwards to an unknown destination. When we had marched to the Somme six months earlier, it was with a sun-tanned, seasoned lot of men. The battalion, as it marched out, made a sorry contrast – men footsore and almost bootless from heavy work in the mud, while their thin, white faces told of the mental and the physical strain they had endured.

At Warloy, we went into billets for the night. Some men had fallen out during the march, and many were on the verge of collapse. During the march, the strong carried the rifles and packs of the weak but, even so, we had to step short and reduce our pace. In billets, the men washed and painted their feet with methylated spirit and picric acid to prevent blisters. After a meal, they walked about the village or sat in the estaminets, while the officers were busy making out our lists of boots, socks and equipment necessary before a long march could be undertaken.

Next day, 20th March, we marched to Puchevillers, where we picked up our band instruments and drums.

On 21st March, we marched to Barley, where we billeted. Every march now saw an improvement in the men's condition. The band, strict march discipline, and no work were doing wonders, whilst mixing with the civilians in the villages, getting vin blanc and omelettes, and plenty of sleep was making the cure complete.

On 22nd and 23rd March, we rested whilst the remainder of the Division concentrated around Ligny. We were marching by stages, about 16 miles a day, via St Pol, Tangry, Auchez-au-Bois and Lillers to Vendin-Les-Bethune, where we arrived on 28th March.

A concentrated march along main routes required strict timing. All units were given starting times and starting points away from the main route to ensure that they arrived in the correct order. So accurate was the timing that each column arrived only a minute or two before the march commenced. At the given second, the unit commanders all along the the line gave the command 'quick march', when the whole column moved off together, marching two and a half miles an hour. At ten minutes to each hour, the line of march halted and the men 'fell out' on the right side of the road, took off their packs, which they sat upon. At a minute to each hour, the order 'get dressed and fall in' was given and, on the hour exactly, the column moved off together again.

Generals and staff officers flew about in cars, taking notes upon march discipline. They tested the distances between the units, and ensured that during halts all mounted personnel dismounted from their horses, that pack animals were relieved of their boxes of ammunition, and that all weight was taken off the shaft horses by using the shaft rest. At no time was any man or animal allowed to impinge upon the left side of the road which was kept clear for two-way traffic.

At the midday halt, men 'fell out' to the right of the road and sat drumming on their mess-tins with their knives and forks, waiting for the meal to arrive. They cheered the cooks as the heavy draught horses dragged the steaming kitchens forward with the midday meal. Messmen lifted the dixies from the mobile fire, and each company formed up in a queue to await their pint of hot stew, which they eked out with the bread ration from their haversacks. When the meal was finished, the dixies were washed out, filled with clean water and put back on the fires to be ready for tea the moment the men arrived in billets.

Our Division and other troops were moving on parallel roads, about one mile apart. When on the march, troops stretched away in front and rear and on either flank as far as the eye could see. First, a succession of infantry battalions, each battalion separated by a gap of fifty yards, and composed of 400 yards of infantry in columns of four, headed by drums or a band, then 200 yards of transport, with four kitchen chimneys sticking up in the air, each sending its own distinct thread of smoke skyward. In the rear of the infantry, came the engineers with their heavy wagons, then the batteries of artillery and ammunition columns and, last of all, either the Army Service Corps supply wagons or the field ambulances. It was a formidable display, set to the rhythm of men's feet marching in time, the metallic sound of the heavy wagons bumping along the uneven roads, and all to the accompaniment of drums and marching bands. It was an expression of military prowess and efficiency that heartened everyone.

Perhaps the most memorable part of any concentration march is arriving into a town at dusk, in an area packed with troops assembled for an offensive. I remember particularly marching into Lillers at dusk. The rear companies had begun to be obscured, and the lights of the town were just coming into their own, as we marched down a slight pave slope between two rows of stone buildings which flung the sound of our drums and of our feet back at us as we marched. The transport wagons rattled along behind us as we swung along to a combined band and bugle marching air which the men were singing. The troops in the estaminets rushed to the windows and the doors and out into the street shouting 'What division?' and 'What battalion?' before giving the final welcome of one lot of attackers to another, 'You're bloody well for it!'

After arranging billets for the night, the men mixed in the estaminets with the men of other divisions. Wonderful stories were told about the Somme, and of the battle that was to come.

15

*'The Green Estaminet' by Sub Lieutenant A P Herbert,
Drake Battalion, RND*

The old men sit by the chimney-piece and drink the good red
   wine
And tell great tales of the Soixante-Dix to the men from the
   English line,
And Madame sits in her old arm-chair and sighs to herself all
   day —
So Madelaine serves the soldiers in the Green Estaminet.
For Madame wishes the War was won and speaks of a strange
   disease,
And Pierre is somewhere about Verdun, and Albert on the seas;
Le Patron, 'e is soldat too, but long time prisonnier —
So Madelaine serves the soldiers in the Green Estaminet.
She creeps downstairs when the black dawn scowls and helps at a
   neighbour's plough,
She racks the midden and feeds the fowls and milks the lonely
   cow,
She mends the holes in the Padre's clothes and keeps his billet
   gay —
And she also serves the soldiers in the Green Estaminet.
The smoke grows thick and the wine flows free and the great
   round songs begin,
And Madelaine sings in her heart, maybe, and welcomes the whole
   world in;
But I know that life is a hard, hard thing, and I know that her lips
   look grey,

Though she smiles as she serves the soldiers in the Green
    Estaminet.
But many a tired young English lad has learned his lesson there,
To smile and sing when the world looks bad, 'for, Monsieur, c'est
    la guerre.'
Has drunk her honour and made his vow to fight in the same
    good way
That Madelaine serves the soldiers in the Green Estaminet.
A big shell came on a windy night, and half of the old house
    went,
But half of the old house stands upright, and Mademoiselle's
    content;
The shells still fall in the square sometimes, but Madelaine means
    to stay,
So Madelaine serves the soldiers still in the Green Estaminet.

[A P Herbert wrote a number of poems and verses etc. during
the war. Some, like 'The Green Estaminet', were published in *The
Bomber Gipsy*, published by Methuen & Co. in 1919. Others were
found in his papers after his death.]

16

The Battle of Gavrelle, April 1917

The Royal Marines at the Gavrelle Windmill, *RND* Issue 3

[After the attack at Miraumont, the RND returned to rest, first around Ovillers, then, by the end of March, in the more familiar areas north-west of Arras.

On 14th April, after yet another period of recovery and reinforcement, the Division moved into the front line at Gavrelle, a small, heavily fortified village on the Arras−Douai road. Today, Gavrelle is not a very inspiring place, but it was a much ghastlier place in 1917. Built on rising ground, it had a windmill on the crest which overlooked the British lines.]

On 23rd April, the 189th and 190th Brigades of the **RND** captured Gavrelle village creating a salient in the German lines, but any advance forward was impossible, as the high ground to the north-east of the village, on which stood a windmill, was still in German hands.

The purpose of the attack on the 28th was as a supporting role to the Canadian Corps attack to the north at Vimy Ridge. The two Royal Marine Battalions were the assault units, C company of Anson providing a flank guard, the Honourable Artillery Company (HAC) in reserve, and Howe and 10th Royal Dublin Fusiliers assigned to carrying duties.

There were to be two separate attacks. The northern attack was to be carried out by 1 RM. The southern attack was to be undertaken by **2 RM**, with a company of Anson suporting.

2 RM would start from within Gavrelle village with two separate objectives – the windmill on high ground to the north-east, and a group of unfinished trenches to the south of the Gavrelle–Izel road.

When the morning battle had finished, and 1 and **2 RM** had consolidated their gains, the plan was for **2 RM** to relieve the Anson company and take over their trenches.

The whole of Anson Battalion would then assault the Germans at Gavrelle to bring the line up to the Marines' line. The southern attack commenced on time at 4.25 a.m. with **2 RM** attacking. The wire was found to be cut in only one place and A, C and D companies of **2 RM** poured through.

At around 5 a.m., C company of Anson moved out but found difficulty virtually immediately, as 400 yards ahead of the front line, near to the Gavrelle–Fresnes road, there was a strongpoint which was resisting with machine-gun and rifle fire.

This was overcome by **2 RM** and, at 7 a.m., it was reported by a wounded man that the windmill and the first trench objectives had been taken and the final objective was under attack.

It was also reported that there was heavy machine-gun fire and sniping from both flanks and, therefore, no information could be sent back. A little later, at 7.25 a.m., it was reported that **2 RM** had taken all of its objectives but had sustained many casualties getting this far.

At 7.30 a.m., Anson were in serious trouble, taking heavy casualties. The defensive series of outposts that were meant to secure **2 RM**'s flank were not in place, leaving **2 RM** exposed to machine-gun fire from both flanks. And there was no sign of 1 RM on their left.

At 8.30 a.m., thirty prisoners were sent down from the windmill. At the same time, final confirmation was received that all objectives had been taken. However, anyone, including stretcher-bearers, who moved into the open was being sniped at or machine-gunned.

The situation stayed like this for an hour or so but, by 10 a.m., Anson, who had suffered badly, had still not secured the **2 RM** flank. Their CO decided to withdraw and all the Anson members came in except for a small force that was too far out to move back. (They managed to withdraw after dark.) This left **2 RM** out in a deep salient with no support on either side and, therefore, in a serious position.

At 10.10, the windmill was counter-attacked by about 150 of the enemy but they were beaten off with the help of the artillery. **2 RM** were now having to withstand a number of counter-attacks, and they had to send out an SOS signal.

Although things were holding up fairly well − except for B company, who couldn't fight their way through the original gap − A, C and D companies of **2 RM** were being drawn into a trap. By 11.58 a.m., another German attack was in the offing as enemy troops were seen massing in the area of **2 RM**'s final objective, the unfinished trenches south of the Gavrelle−Izel road. This was again broken up by artillery. A fair portion of the cut-off companies were forced to surrender.

At 2.10 p.m., the Germans massed again to the east of Gavrelle and yet again the artillery saved the day. At 2.30 p.m., the CO of **2 RM** conceded that his men were now holding only the old German front line and the Windmill, which had been reinforced. In addition, some men were cut off in the area south of the Gavrelle−Izel road.

The Germans commenced another attack on the Windmill, which was repulsed with heavy casualties. In all, the enemy massed to attack on three more occasions, each time the artillery broke up the advance. The Germans launched one final attack on **2 RM** at 8.30 p.m. but again, with the help of the artillery, it was beaten off.

Now the 14th Worcesters came up, taking over the line of the Anson and **2 RM**, which signified the end of the attacks on the southern front.

Needless to say, the attack scheduled for later in the day by Anson was cancelled.

Casualties, 2 Btn RMLI:
Officers: 6 killed, 3 taken prisoner.

Other ranks: 155 killed, 157 wounded (5 of whom died of their wounds), 28 taken prisoner.

2 Btn RMLI had also taken 30 casualties on the run up to the attack.

[**2 Btn RMLI** casualties given in this article are, according to the author, virtually 100 per cent accurate, as he can put a name to them all; but he has been unable to get a definite figure for the strength of the battalion when it set out. He speculates around 500, as in the Battle of the Ancre, so that **2 Btn RMLI** was practically wiped out. My father, who was in 'A' Company **2 Btn RMLI**, was obviously lucky to survive.]

John Brough, Royal Marine 1914/1919.

Photographs of extant Brough connections with North York Moors.

Top left: Tombstone of his grandparents, Thomas and Hannah Brough, churchyard of St Peter's and St Paul's, Pickering.
Top right: Roll of Honour, St John's church, Newton-upon-Rawcliffe.
Below: Cottage at Goathland built by his uncle John, a stonemason, slab with date and Brough initial.

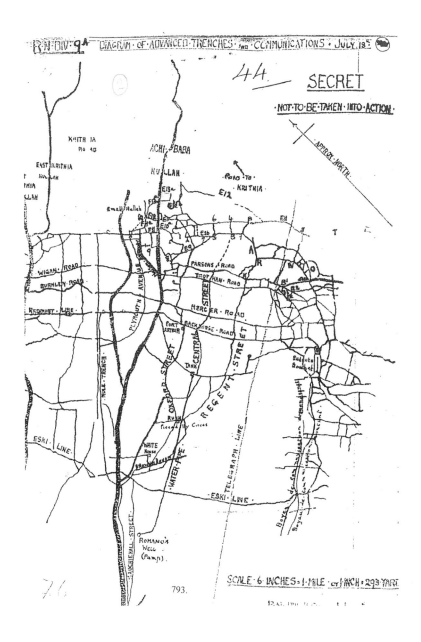

Diagram of the trenches, Battle of Achi Baba. Copied from *RND*.

PORT SAID. FERDINAND DE LESSEPS.

Following my father from his postcards.

Returning from the Dardanelles, 1915.
Reverse reads: 'Mon July 24. I expect
you will be wondering how I am getting
on. Well, I am almost well again now,
so you need not worry about me. I hope
you are well at home and having a fine

summer. Is Tom with you now? I wonder if you got that letter I sent, also
the postcard, and I haven't had any news from you of a long time, but, still, I
expect to be coming to England soon, so it can wait. This is the statue of the
man who made the Suez Canal. Your ever loving son, John.'

Following my father from his postcards.

Above: Christmas Day 1915. Florrie Pickering was 'the girl next door'. Her father Nathan's farm, Fowlpot, adjoined Wethead.
Left: Awaiting embarkation for France, September 1916. To his brother Tom.

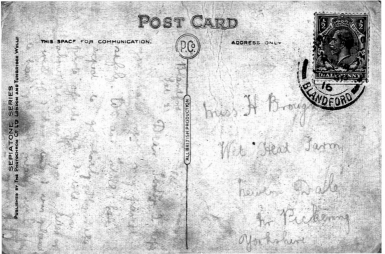

Following my father from his postcards.

Above: Awaiting embarkation for France, September 1916, sent to his sister. Reverse message reads:

'Blandford, Sat 21(9/16)
Dear Sister, I hope you have got my parcel safety. We are still here, expect to go shortly. This is the photo of the YMCA I told you about.
I shall send you a letter if I have time. I was pleased to hear that you were nearly well again. Yours JB'

Following my father from his postcards.

Christmas Card 1916.
Message on reverse reads 'With best wishes from John wishing you the best of New Year's greetings to you all at home'.

Postcard to his mother, reads 'Just a PC to tell you we have arrived part of our way on our journey, are embarking in a few minutes so haven't time for much correspondence, so good-bye for the time. It is time to fall in now so shall have to be off. Your ever loving son, John'.
Seems he had no time to post his card.

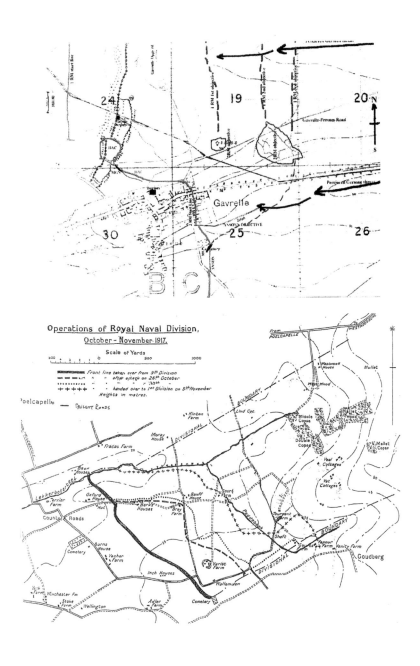

Above: Map of Royal Marines attack at Gavrelle. Copied from *RND*
Below: Map of Battle of Passchendaele, 26 October – 5 November 1917.
Copied from *RND*

17

The Battle of Passchendaele, 26th October to 5th November 1917

RND *Issue 22*

The village of Passchendaele remains a haunting memory of where so many **RND** lost their lives for about 1000 yards of sodden earth.

The Division was relieved in the Oppy-Gavrelle sector on 26th September 1917, and proceeded to the Villars Chattel area for a period of 14 days' training prior to being engaged in the Flanders battle. However, two days later, the Division was railed to Flanders and the training programme cancelled.

The Division was called upon to fight three battles, each of one brigade strength. It was decided to use the **188th Infantry Brigade** first, then the 189th and, lastly, the 190th, as this brigade was most in need of training. The troops were accordingly disposed in the new area, with **188th Brigade** being located in Dirty Bucket Camp nearest the front.

On 4th October, information was received that the Division would, after all, be given 14 days' training, although one brigade was required immediately to work in the forward area for about a week. 189th was chosen for this duty as it was not due to go into action until after the **188th**, and was less in need of training than the 190th.

The **188th** and 189th Brigades accordingly exchanged camps on 6th October, 189th moving forward to Dirty Bucket camp and **188th** being withdrawn to the Herzeele area.

Until they moved to the forward area on 23rd October, **188th**

Brigade carried out intensive training. Definite instructions for the attack having been received on 18th October, they were able to train for the capture of specific objectives. Each battalion made a large scale model of the area to be attacked. Much ingenuity was shown in the construction of these models, and they were visited daily by many of the men, in their spare time, to discuss their various tasks.

On 19th October, having been informed that the first day on which the Division would be required to fight was 26th October, application was made to move into position on [the] night of 24th/25th. This would allow the assault troops the maximum amount of time to continue training, whilst assuring them of a complete day in the front line in which to get their bearings.

188th moved by bus route on 23rd October to the forward area. On 24th October, they took over the front line from 27th Infantry Brigade without incident – Anson Battalion on the right, 1st Royal Marines on the left, **2nd Royal Marines** in support and Howe Battalion in reserve.

In the attack, Anson Battalion on the right and 1st Royal Marines on the left were to capture the first objectives, closely followed by Howe Battalion and **2nd Royal Marines**, who would pass through them on the line of the first objectives and attack and consolidate the second objectives. On the right, where the ground was slightly higher and more opposition was expected, Anson Battalion were given a frontage of 550 yards; 1st Royal Marines, on the left, where the ground was boggy, and only lightly held by the enemy, were allotted a frontage of 1000 yards.

The 25th October and night 25th/26th were brilliantly fine but, at 3.30 a.m. on the 26th, the weather suddenly broke and rain was continuous throughout the day. The already heavy going was made considerably worse

The attack was launched at 5.40 a.m. Two minutes later, the enemy put down a barrage exactly on the line as anticipated. As the troops had been assembled in front of this line, little damage was done by the enemy fire and the advance was not checked.

7.12 a.m. wounded men of Anson Battalion reported that the attack was going satisfactorily up to the third lift of the barrage.

7.20 a.m. reported that Howe Battalion had captured Varlet Farm after a stiff fight. In fact, it was a concrete pill-box some 200 yards further east – Varlet Farm no longer existed except for a few scattered bricks, and all the farm buildings had completely disappeared. Other points of reference on the map, such as Source Trench and the farm moat, were indistinguishable because of the many flooded shell holes, all of which caused a great deal of confusion.

7.26 a.m. Anson Battalion reported that they had pushed on through Wallemolen and reached the wire at Source Trench, but no report had been received of the trench being taken.

7.30 a.m. 1st Royal Marines reported wounded coming back and that the first objective had been taken. Half an hour later, a pigeon message, despatched 6.40 a.m., from 1st Royal Marines stated Banff House captured and a position 150 yards in front of it being consolidated.

8.25 a.m. as far as was known, 1st Royal Marines were still consolidating 150 yards beyond Banff House, and Anson Battalion had reached the south end of Source Trench and taken Varlet Farm after much bayonet fighting.

9 a.m. report received from wounded men of Howe Battalion that the Paddebeek Stream had been reached, and 1st Royal Marines reported that **2nd Royal Marines** had passed through with slight casualties.

Very little information had been received from the left sector. The OC of **2nd Royal Marines** was asked to hasten his report. The situation of the Marine Battalions was unclear. 1st Royal Marines had gained their objectives in the west but were still held up in the centre just east of the Wallemolen–Bray Farm Road. Very little information had been received from the left sector. With practically no news of **2nd Royal Marines**, it was thought that they were held up on the same line, where their companies were now intermixed with those of 1st Royal Marines.

When communication was established, they were told of the urgent need to press forward, as the enemy were enfilading the Division's troops south of Source Trench.

Towards nightfall, OC 1st Royal Marines reported that his troops had been forced to withdraw from Banff House and now held Berks Houses as their most advanced post.

Later information regarding the left battalion, **2nd Royal Marines**, was that they had moved forward in accordance with operational orders. The leading platoons, from statements of survivors, appear to have reached the Paddebeek and crossed it to the south-east. Coming under heavy machine-gun fire, they later withdrew to the west. It was reported that great numbers were killed in attempting to cross the stream and that bodies of many men of **2nd Royal Marines** were seen lying along the line of it. Orders were issued for **2nd Royal Marines** to re-occupy the positions at Banff House and Bray Farm that night. This was only partially achieved.

So the first day came to an end.

The RND continued in the offensive up until 5th November. **188th Brigade** remained in the line for a further two days after this, being relieved 7th/8th November. The Division then withdrew to the Lederzeele training area.

Casualties suffered were:

188th Brigade

216 killed	776 wounded	4 gassed	216 missing

189th Brigade

14 killed	82 wounded	54 gassed	3 missing

190th Brigade

219 killed	599 wounded	1 gassed	140 missing

18

Some Recollections of Gallipoli and the Western Front,
Brigadier Basil Rackham

RND *Issue 17*

Aboard SS Franconia *en route Gallipoli, October 1915*
The officers had excellent accommodation, but the men were very crowded. We found our food to be first class but, for the other ranks, it was not so good. In those days, there was a great gulf between officer and man.

Ashore at Gallipoli
The other ranks had a much harder life than the officers except on the Peninsula, where everybody was on the same level. I think this was good as all the veneer was off and you saw through to the person himself, stripped of all class problems. Although there was still this gulf between officer and man, this never disappeared.

Western Front, France. Battle of the Ancre, 13th November 1916
At night, there were thousands of us out in the open waiting for the attack. If the Germans had known that, and concentrated their artillery on us, there would have been terrible slaughter.

There was a German strongpoint which had not been dealt with by the gunners or the leading troops and you could see the Germans manning it. Actually, I saw one shooting at me and I dropped down. Unfortunately, my batman, situated behind me, caught the bullet and fell onto me, dying in the process.

We couldn't do much all that day. Two tanks were brought up, and I think the Germans were so frightened of the tanks that they simply surrendered. Two or three hundred were captured when this strongpoint was mopped up; it had done amazing damage to our battalions which had come up against it.

Winter of 1917

After the Battle of the Ancre we had to go back into reserve to obtain reinforcements. We came back into the line again at the same place – just above Beaucourt – this was in early February 1917. This was the coldest winter we have ever had, it was terrible. There wasn't really a front-line like a continuous trench, just little holes. You just couldn't dig anymore, the ground was as hard as bricks. This made us vulnerable and as a result we had considerable casualties.

April 1917 Gavrelle

Gavrelle, in the Arras area, was soon after the assault by the Canadians at Vimy Ridge. The Division obtained its objectives, an advance of about a couple of miles, the capture of the village and the windmill so we could consolidate.

October 1917 Passchendaele

I don't often talk about my experiences in the First World War but, whenever I do, I always say that there was nothing so dreadful as Passchendaele. The conditions there were beyond description, it never ought to have been. Mud, mud, mud – if you slipped you were sunk. Passchendaele was inhuman.

19

From My Father's Diary, Taken POW

[My father's original diary is in the archives of the Royal Marines Museum at Southsea. It is not a printed diary but a hardback notebook, opening upwards, about four inches wide and six inches long. The first page reads:

Pte J. Brough **RMLI**,
A Coy, 2nd Royal Marine Bn,
B.E.F. France.
A present from Tom, Sept 26, 1917, while on leave to England.

Probably on compassionate leave following the death of his mother, Mary Jane Brough, buried at Newton-upon-Rawcliffe, 13th September 1917. His father had died in March of that year.

There are some blanks in the diary and, unfortunately, no entries for the last six months of his captivity.]

The following is a report of my doings since I was captured on the 26th October 1917 till the following year.

John Brough

26th October, Friday
Went over the top at Passchendaele Ridge. The attack commenced at dawn. The ground was very unfavourable for us as it had been raining the night before. The whole attack was a failure owing to the ground being so muddy. Nearly all our fellows got wounded or

killed, including the officer in charge, Mr [illegible]. We went too far and so got surrounded by the enemy. Stayed in the shell holes till 12 noon then tried to get back but without success so got ...

[pages missing]

30th Oct, Tues
... is not a very warm place, hope we shall be moving away soon, I am tired of being a prisoner. It came on to rain about dinnertime and is bitterly cold, continued to rain all afternoon.

31st Oct, Wed
Much warmer this morning. I heard our aeroplanes dropping bombs somewhere not far off during the night. I haven't had a wash since I was taken prisoner so am feeling a bit dirty and in need of a shave and a change of clothes. We had straw to sleep on last night, it was much better. Went on a fatigue just before dinner and, after, had a half-hour's platoon drill in front of the German officers. Been a fine day.

1st Nov, Thurs
We are doing our own cooking today. Had a rather sleepless night but not cold – too crushed for that – 60 of us in a very small room, packed in like sardines, in fact, it's the Black Hole of Calcutta! Nothing of importance occurred today. Been fine but cold.

2nd Nov, Fri
It was a misty and cold, wet morning. I did not sleep very well feeling a bit slutty now without a change of clothes or a wash. It would be better if we could get our clothes off at night but no blankets have been issued as yet. We are not too well dealt with by the Germans but the Belgiums are very good to us and throw us turnips and tobacco as they pass. Been captured a week now, seems more like a year to me. We had a very good dinner today made by

our own cooks. I think the vegetables were a present from the Belgium people. It has been a dull, misty day. Had soup at night in place of coffee, had the same last night. The bread is very different from our English, being very sour and brown or, rather, black. Had jam last night. Two loaves between five persons. I haven't seen any soap since I arrived, wish I was back!

3rd Nov, Sat
It was a very fine day. Just before dinner, about 10.30, the corporal of the German Intelligence came over to the 63rd Division men for them to get ready to move at once. It left eight of us and we got ready and marched about three miles to the station where we took the train for our new place. Kortrijk it is called. As we passed through Roulers we noticed much damage done by our airmen, all the houses are in ruins, so I would think it has had a good many bombs dropped. We had a good bowl of soup as soon as we arrived, then another about one hour afterwards with coffee after that, so we did not do so bad. Later on, we had our particulars taken then a couple of blankets given to each. We had beds to sleep on made of shavings inside a brown paper ticking, it was much better than the night previous.
[Kortrijk and Roulers (Flemish Roeselare) are in W. Belgium.]

4th Nov, Sun
Got up about seven o'clock. Had hot coffee for breakfast then went for a bath and our clothes fumigated – the only thing is, there is no soap anywhere here. I left a lot in my pack, don't I just wish I had it now! And a towel to dry with – we had to stay in a hot room till we were dry and our clothes ready for use again. A lot of Germans were bathing at the same time, they all do the same here. Anyhow, I am pleased we got moved here. Still, it's a little dreary not being allowed out after our baths. We are placed in a room, the eight of us, for sleeping. I am pleased we are all together still as we have been so all along. Not much special to report – could do with a shave. Wrote a letter home and one postcard.

5th Nov, Mon

Got up in haste to go to the WC. Had hot coffee for break-fast. Weather cold this morning but kept fine all day. Some more prisoners came today, just captured this morning. Got a nice warm stove to sit over. I suppose we shall be moving away as soon as they get a few more captures. I got a letter-card given today. Took a bucket up with us tonight so that we shall be all right. Had a very good romp around today, bought some kind of substance called cheese, had it with the black bread we use. Went to bed at nine.

6th Nov, Tues

Got up at seven after a very nice, comfortable night. There seems to be a heavy barrage on this morning, we could hear the guns quite distinctly from our prison. Began about 6.30 a.m., continued for three hours or more. During the evening, some of our aeroplanes were about not far off. The German anti-aircraft guns were boom-ing them without success. It began to rain around dinnertime but eventually faired up after dark. I began to write a letter to Mrs Baker but did not get it finished.

7th Nov, Wed

There was a small barrage on again this morning but nothing compared with yesterday's. It came on to rain and was a regular wet day but faired up at night. There was an air-raid on this place. One bomb dropped just outside the prison and properly put the wind up us all, knocking all the lights out (this place is lit with electricity). This occurred just after 8 p.m. I heard them about during the night – not much hope for us should one drop here as we are locked in over night.

8th Nov, Thurs

The guard did not let us out till 8 a.m. this morning. After break-fast, went and swept up the broken glass from outside the prison. My, but there were a lot of broken windows! Not one was un-broken on the front side where the bomb dropped. Very cold morning but fine. Got the lights on again tonight. Stagg got a pack of cards so had a game of whist at night. Stagg is one of the men captured along with me, also belonging to the Marines. Sent a postcard to the Bakers at Whitby today. Had a very peaceful night.

9th Nov, Fri

Got up at the same time. After breakfast, swept out our cell then had a good game of cards till dinnertime and also afterwards. Just after tea, we were all called down below and certain of us were told off to move in the morning. All out of this room were told off: I am pleased as they are a lot of very very nice fellows, all Royal Marines except one who is in the London Rifle Brigade. Heard a few of our aeroplanes knocking about at night. Very fine day.

10th Nov, Sat

Got up about seven. Had breakfast and got a little more bread together with jam as we are moving today, 28 of us all told, the lot RMs. Got in the same train. Stood at a place called Dendermonde for the night. All the … from the school … were here. Slept … Belgium place, just about crowded out with 120 or so. As we came along we saw some very interesting sights … at Ghent St Peter. Very wet day, moving again tomorrow.

11th Nov, Sun

Got up and had breakfast of hot coffee and bread with a sausage, the first meat I've tasted since being captured. We were then marched off and put in trucks, forty of us. There was a stove and seats. Got 10 marks for my jerkin, bought one mark of apples to eat on our way to Germany. Travelled in cattle trucks and stayed at the several stations for hours. Got some food at 8 a.m. but nothing since beginning our journey. We were almost dead with hunger and cold. Came on to rain.

12th Nov, Mon

After a rough night without much sleep found we were still in

Belgium. Most miserable ride I've done. We had a stove in the truck but it did not give off much heat and we had a lot of bumping and shunting. Just crossed the border about eight o'clock tonight. I am properly fed up with this bumping about all day and all we got to eat was one bowl of soup at night and a quarter of a loaf for the whole day. Was a very fine day.

13th Nov, Tues
We arrived at our destination about two o'clock in the afternoon. Had a good way to march from the station. Got all our clothes fumigated and a wash. Changed my money into German but, while in the bath, someone stole the purse and the lot, £2 in all. Got some very poor soup, worse than pig-swill. Had a couple of warm blankets and a bed to sleep in. No food was issued to us all day except for two very small slices of bread on the station where we were stopped for a long time. Very wild and cold looking place. Beautiful day.

14th Nov, Wed
Got up at six. After a very cold night had nothing again for breakfast except a very poor drop of coffee. Had an issue of postcards, sent one to Hannah [his sister]. Feeling fit for a good meal, it's a couple of days since we had anything so am about dead beat. After dinner, which consisted of cabbage water, we were served out with a parcel each, a gift through the Red Cross Society. They were packed with three tins of bully, three tins of milk, one packet of tea, one packet of cocoa, two tins of cheese, one tin of dripping and four packets of biscuits – so we all sat down to a right good feed! Ten of us dipped our bread at tea-time so the parcel came in useful.

15th Nov, Thurs
Got up at about the same time after a very good night's rest, was quite warm last night. We have a full room now and a nice warm fire. Did not do much except play cards and eat biscuits, just about finished my lot now. Got served out with a roll of white bread

this morning, one roll between three men. A very fine, sunny day. Very poor soup for dinner. When we emptied the slops, the Italian prisoners outside our camp came for the spare and ate it like like a pack of wolves − poor beggars, it's a pity to see them starve. Went for bread again at night. Got the few photos back that were taken [stolen with his purse, etc.]. Decided to turn in early tonight. Vaccinated and inoculated this afternoon, three of the first, one of the second. Haven't heard anything of my purse but have made enquiries, I suppose the guards have got it, the thugs!

16th Nov, Fri
Got up at the same time. Had coffee for breakfast. A lot of our fellows are ill today, think the inoculations are taking effect. Stagg is not at all well so did not get a game of cards today. My parcel is getting low now. I went for the … Been a rather dull, cold day. For dinner we had black peas and water with fishbones and didn't they smell! The fish, I mean. For tea we had gruel, which was much better and, with a little milk, made it a treat. The lights went out early tonight, about 6.30. Haven't done very much yet. We only get two slices of black bread each man from the Germans.

17th Nov, Sat
Got up at the same time. Had coffee for breakfast and also finished off my second tin of cheese. My goodness, it's three years since I joined the Marines, who would have thought I should be here to celebrate the third anniversary of it. Wish we could get some books to read. After dinner, we subscribed around and got a postcard each − I wrote mine to Hannah. There were no lights on again tonight so had to turn in the dark. Was a very cold day. About 52 prisoners landed here today. Had soup for tea but no bread issue till morning. Feeling very hungry, used a second bully today.

18th Nov, Sun
Had to get up in the dark again. Had cocoa for breakfast then fell in for muster afterwards and given our prisoner numbers, mine is

47097. Stagg was a good deal better and acted as tailor and sewed them on for our hut. Got our two slices of bread and an issue of jam, one spoonful per man. They don't believe in over-feeding here! Cold, raw day, very much like snow. I heard from our fellows who came in yesterday that our men now occupy the whole of the Passchendaele Ridge, was pleased with this news. Got served out with a paper and envelope. My last tin of bully went west tonight. The lights were on tonight.

19th Nov, Mon
After breakfast of coffee and black bread, fell in for the usual muster and had the martial law read over to us. I was busy during the morning writing a letter to Florrie [Pickering]. The paper and envelope were served out yesterday. It was a very dull, cold day. Dinner was black peas and water, just a trifle better than before. I am just about ready for the next parcel. We do not work here, have three blankets and good coconut matting beds, so cannot grumble. Had a drop of fish rounds soup for tea.

20th Nov, Tues
Got up a bit late. Had some kind of oatmeal for breakfast which was not half bad. For dinner, we had cabbage and beans and, for tea, pearl barley. I was unlucky again tonight and got none, together with about forty more, and so, in consequence, made a big hole into tomorrow's bread; I have one slice left for all day, roll on the next parcel! We were inoculated again this afternoon, it did not take long to do us all. Wish they would feed us instead of sticking needles into us! My, what a life this is, wish I was back with the battalion. Hope to move soon.

21st Nov, Wed
Did not get up till late as we had no lights in our hut this morning. Had coffee for breakfast. It was a very wet morning but faired up towards dinnertime. Had cabbage for dinner. Expect we are moving into the Italian camp. Had our particulars taken – colour of eyes,

100

weight, height, etc. Hoping to get a parcel again on Saturday, could do with one now I have opened my last tin of milk. We moved to Group 2 this afternoon, gave our blankets and bowls in before we left, served out with some more as soon as we got there.

22nd Nov, Thurs
Had a sleepless night, couldn't sleep for fleas, they were coming out of the things they call blankets like swarms of bees. The blankets are very thin and small. I am not in the same hut as my pals but got the hut next to them. Got a tablet of soap from the canteen and, as soon as the water came on, had a good wash. One very small piece costs twopence here, takes a lot of rubbing to make a lather. Was a very fine day. Had a much better dinner – cabbage and beans. Had coffee for breakfast and fish rounds for soup tonight. We were inoculated again today, they think we are pin-cushions!

23rd Nov, Fri
I didn't sleep well last night, the … in the … were too busy. Had a wash and walk round. Did not feel up to much today, had a headache. Made a cup of cocoa during the morning. It was a dull day and cold. Martinmas day in the old country. We are all looking forward to a parcel; need it, too, as we only got coffee for breakfast. Got a good fire going today. Roll on peace! Bought a purse yesterday. One month since I was captured – seems a year. Had a very good dinner of beans and cabbage. Been making cocoa all day, finished my last tin of milk.

24th Nov, Sat
Got up about seven. No lights being on, I slept in and missed the coffee, I did not mind that at all. I made myself pass the morning on by playing draughts with a chap from Bradford. After dinner, which was a decent meal, made some cocoa and again after tea which was black soup. I hate the soup, we had it the first day we came here, some of them line up for it all the same. The lights went off tonight about six. Did not get any parcel, some think … Had a very good fire. Fine but cold day, very much like rain.

25th Nov, Sun
Got up at seven after a sleepless night. Had cocoa for breakfast but it was nearly cold. Very dark morning and been a regular stormy night. No lights again this morning. After breakfast, was served out with a spoonful of jam per man. Got served out with a postcard, I sent mine to Hannah. Saw my purse today, one of the Frenchmen had it, been sold to him for two biscuits by one of our fellows. Tried to trace him out but without success. The devils, can't trust your own countrymen! Very wet, stormy day. Lights went off early. Had barley for tea, very thin. Turned in early tonight.

26th Nov, Mon
Got up rather late and just got coffee in time, awful stuff it was. My, how cold it was today – no fire, nearly frozen all night. No parcels were issued today and no coal, so had no fire again tonight. I ate my slice of bread yesterday so had nothing till dinner when we had cabbage and water. For tea, we had salt fish rounds and water. I ate my slice of bread tonight, expect to have a parcel tomorrow. Been a very cold day but fine. I wish I was back on our old rations again, to think of all the bully and biscuits wasted in the battalion while we starve!
P.S. the lights kept in tonight.

27th Nov, Tues
Got up and had some gruel for breakfast, a kind of maize meal. It was a very cold day. We had no coal for the fire so turned in again as it is much warmer in bed. Living in hope of a parcel but none came today. For lunch, had cabbage and water; for tea, some gruel, very nice it was, the best we have had since coming here. Got an issue of coke and coal tonight so we had a nice warm fire to heat the room. It came on a lot warmer towards night. No lights again tonight so turned in early. Not much to report.

28th Nov, Wed
I did not get up for breakfast as it was only coffee and I had eaten

all my bread the previous night, so lay in till roll-call. We went and drew overcoats and got our numbers sewn on. Saw a chum who had been captured at Gavrelle and he gave me some of his parcel. Poor lad, he has lost one arm, a very nice fellow. Got a bit more coal today so kept the fire in all day. Had a game of draughts with my pal Jack Harker. Got inoculated again! Also was served out with half a parcel per man so had a good feed. Made some Quaker oats tonight, very good, too. Came on damp at night.

[Gavrelle: Belgium, NE of Arras]
29th Nov, Thurs
Got up for roll-call but not for coffee. Had a few biscuits for break-fast and made a basin of tea afterwards. Went to a church service at 10 a.m. and enjoyed it very much. Had a very good dinner, better than usual. Bought a tablet of soap and had a wash, also washed a towel and handkerchief. I did not get much sleep last night − it was so very stuffy and hot − so think I will not eat so much tonight, but everyone was the same. Feeling a bit chalky now and fit for another bath and fumigation. It was a very fine and mild day. Made some rice for supper and some cocoa as well. It was not much good, like yeast − still, it came in welcome. My biscuits have all gone now, thought it best to use them as there is a lot of pinching done here, things are lost right and left.

30th Nov, Fri
I did not bother to get up till roll-call then had a walk round and saw my pal. He came over to see me and gave me a tablet of soap and a slice of bread, very good of him, I thought. We had cabbage for dinner and some kind of fish, and it didn't half stink! I made some tea and, for supper, I made some rice and it cooked beauti-fully. I went to bed satisfied for once. I have enough for two more cookings. There are so many wanting tastes! We signed for another parcel today, expect to get it tomorrow. Been a very fine day. I saw another fellow today who was captured last April, Cussack by name. No lights tonight.

1st Dec, Sat
Did not get up till roll-call then opened my tin of cheese and ate the lot to a slice of bread which I had given to me yesterday. I had a wash with real soap today, first time since I was taken prisoner (not first wash, but the first real soap I've used!). It came on wet at night so did not get an issue of parcels, expect to get them on Monday. Nothing of importance occurred today. Got a good stock of coal in for Sunday. No lights again tonight. I used my other tin of bully beef tonight. Feeling very tired, will turn in early.

2nd Dec, Sun
Got up for cocoa – we have cocoa on a Sunday. Went to church at nine o'clock. My, what a day, cold enough for Christmas. After dinner, it started to rain and snow, a regular blizzard. I did not go out far today. Am about eaten up now. We had an issue of jam today. I made some rice for supper but not much cop. Got a post-card served out and sent it to Hannah. No lights again today, this is a most miserable place for lights. I wonder what they are doing now at home, wish I was there with them.

3rd Dec, Mon
I got up in good time as we had some kind of maize gruel for breakfast. It was a very cold day and snow on the ground about 2′ deep after a very cold night. Just before dinner, my friend out of Group 1 came over and brought me some jam and a slice of black bread, he's the best-hearted lad I've met. Got served out with a full parcel just before dinner. Most of the fellows had some bad biscuits but mine were all fairly good. I have a right full parcel now, almost flowing over!
P.S. shifted to Group 1.

4th Dec, Tues
We shifted to Group 1 last night and were placed in no.10 barrack, a very nice room. All are NCOs except the ten of us who moved in last night. Got a bath and fumigated before we moved over. It was

a cold day and snowed like anything yesterday. Today we were on fatigues unloading a truck of potatoes. Had to work hard, did not get finished till 8 p.m., it was quite dark and frosty. Saw quite a crowd of new prisoners in today, about 1500 or so. Had some very good soup tonight. Turned in early, tired out.

5th Dec, Wed

Got up just after reveille. After breakfast, fell in for roll-call and had a fatigue carting coal to the different groups. It was not such a hard job today but did not finish till 5 p.m. Got some lovely soup tonight, barley – very thick, and a good bowlful. The NCOs in our barrack do not bother to draw the German food, they get enough with their parcels. It was a very fine day but cold, the snow is still on the ground, very hard.

6th Dec, Thurs

Got up at roll-call. Was detailed for a fatigue along the railway leading a truck of heather and carrying loads of it from a wood nearby. It was a very cold job and not so easy. After dinner, we got a job along the same road by the munition factory levelling some sand. It was not a hard job but rather cold. They don't half make us work here. At night, I went to the theatre as I had a ticket given, it was very good. Been thawing.

7th Dec, Fri

I got up in right good time and made some tea and, later on, some cocoa before roll-call. Was detailed for a job up at the railway station placing traps round one of the parcel huts so that the rats could not get into the parcels, it was a very good job. At dinnertime, we moved out of no.10 hut into no.9 and a lot more of the old boys are here, too. Not half as good a hut as no.10. Been thawing during the day, very cold night, wet. No lights tonight.

8th Dec, Sat

Got up for coffee and, at roll-call, was detailed for a job levelling sand round by the German barracks — it was not such a very bad job but cold. After dinner, which was cabbage and water, we fell in but were told to go back to the barrack as we were not wanted this afternoon. I went to the barber's for a shave and haircut. For tea, we had barley and it was very good. No lights again tonight except for an old acetylene lamp and it casts a very poor light. Been a fine day.

9th Dec, Sun
Got up at reveille and had cocoa for breakfast and then fell in for roll-call. Was dismissed with nothing to do all day. Went to a church service at 10 a.m. in the next barracks. After dinner, had a walk around, borrowed a book from the library. Got a postcard and letter ready for tomorrow — the postcard I sent to Florrie [Pickering] and the letter to Mrs Baker at Whitby. No lights were on tonight except for the old acetylene. I went to the church at night and it was a good service. Been a fine day.

10th Dec, Mon
Got up at reveille and had coffee for breakfast. At roll-call, gave in our letters and postcards. Was told off for a fatigue round by the hospital emptying the latrines and such like. Was on the same job in the afternoon but only had a short journey so was finished by 2.30 p.m. Was served out with another half parcel tonight. A lot of the boys were told off for a draft that is off away tomorrow. My pal Jack Harker is one and all out of this barrack are going. Been a very fine day, like summer. No lights again tonight.

11th Dec, Tues
The lights were on by 3.30 a.m. for the fellows who are off away today. For breakfast we had black gruel — or cement — most horrible stuff to eat. When the draft had gone we got up. Fell in at roll-call but dodged the work parades. Went round and made some exchanges with the French for my tinned fruit. Also did a bit of washing to pass the time along. After dinner, we were told off for a

fatigue smashing up tins at the station, not such a bad job but rather cold.

12th Dec, Wed
A lot from our barrack went away this morning at 5 a.m. I got up at reveille and made myself some breakfast. At roll-call was detailed off for a fatigue turning over a heap of manure and gathering all the … and such like. After dinner, we were told off for the next draft which is off away in the morning. Served out with a clean change of clothes, then we were inspected by the doctor. Stagg is going with this draft. Leaving Dulmen at 5 a.m. in the morning.

13th Dec, Thurs
Got up at four and had some coffee, got our blankets and bowls and towels and handed them in, then fell in for moving off about 6 a.m. Had a long march to the station — not Dulmen station but Holton. Had to change at Wanner, got to our destination about 10 a.m. It is a mining place with the pit in the rear of our barrack. We are the only English here, the rest are Russian and French. They did not expect us and, therefore, had a lot of humping about. Got a drop of soup for dinner but did not get a very good bed.

14th Dec, Fri
Got up at 10 a.m. Had some coffee and soup then fell in for a kit issue — got served out with a working rig and, after dinner, was sent down a mine! I did not care for this work as I have never been used to it before. Going up and down in the cage was the worst. I was put on a job running trucks, it was fairly hard work. When we had finished at ten (from 2 p.m. to 10 p.m. are the hours we work) had a bath as soon as we came up. Wish I could get out of it, I don't like it at all. We sleep alone in the hut.

[The places he mentions above are all in the former Prussian province of Westphalia, North-West Germany, which in 1945 became North-Rhine Westphalia:

- Dulmen: small town, present population about 9000. 17 miles SW of Munster.
- Haltern (Holton): rail junction, present population about 10,000.
- Wanna-Eickel (Wanner): city of approximately 85,000. Coal mining centre. Formed in 1926 through the incorporation of Wanna and Eickel.]

15th Dec, Sat

When I came off last night Stagg had made my bed down. He went on from 6 a.m. to 2 p.m. I slept in till about ten then got our issue of bread. After dinner, went to work again. I was on a better job helping to get up some rails they run the trucks on. It was a cold, snowy day outside today. Got back about eleven as it takes a long time to get washed and changed. Turned in and had a good sleep. Feeling properly done up not being used to this kind of work. Don't I just wish the war was over!

16th Dec, Sun

Got up at ten but had some coffee earlier. Got our bread issued then fell in for dinner. We did not go to work today and I am glad, I would rather be in Dulmen now. They say we get paid 1 mark per shift, and we earn it, too! It was a nasty snowy day, very cold, and I did not turn out much. It is quite warm down the pit — it's a coal pit, by the way — and doesn't half give me a headache, and backache, too! There are a lot of German women employed on the top. A party of our fellows refused to work today and had to stand outside all the afternoon. Sent a postcard home.

17th Dec, Mon

Got up at 4 a.m., had some coffee, then set off for the pit about 5.30 a.m. I had a job just inside the pit bottom running trucks along to the shaft with a Frenchman, it was an easy job and we did not hurry ourselves. We are on the day shift this week. When we got back, drew our bread and soup. Later, in the evening, got some hot water and made myself some cocoa to go down the pit with in the morning. Stagg is on afternoons this week. Been a cold day and rather wet.

18th Dec, Tues

Got up at four and had breakfast then fell in for the pit. I was on a very nasty job unloading stone and such like, it was difficult as I could not straighten my back at all. I am getting a bit more into the way of the pit now, especially the cage — did not like it at all, and don't yet for that matter, but shall do in time, I hope. Not being able to understand the German language makes it twice as hard as it would be. It has been a lovely day but cold.

19th Dec, Wed

Up at 4 a.m., got ready and went to the pit. We went down on our own this morning thinking to see the boy at the bottom but did not, so set off by ourselves and got lost in the pit but, at last, got right and made a start. I was on the same job, shovelling the stone into the place the coal had been got out of — filling in, I suppose, they call it. It has been a lovely day but very frosty. It is nice and warm down in the mine. Getting a bit more used to it now.

20th Dec, Thurs

Being on mornings this week I got up at 4 a.m. Got ready and fell in for the pit. We waited for our guide this morning as it is not safe getting all over the place same as yesterday. I had the same job but a much pleasanter German to work with. There is a great deal of difference in them, some are very nice fellows. Had a very good day today. Much colder and much like snow. Been here a week now.

21st Dec, Fri

Got up at 4 a.m., had some coffee then set off for the pit. Had a rather hard morning's work and felt jolly tired by the time 2 p.m. came. The food we get is not sufficient to keep up our constitutions for the work we have to do. I have seen a difference in the boys since we began work in the mine. It was a very cold and frosty day, a very ideal Christmas season. This is not a nice place, we are not allowed to go out at all. Stagg is here but on afternoons shift. He is only a skeleton of his former self.

22nd Dec, Sat
Got up at 4 a.m. Warmed up some cabbage soup for breakfast then got ready and went off to the pit. Had a nice easy job today, that is, if there is an easy one anywhere down the pit. I managed to take some lunch down and it came in all right. We are not going down again till 10 p.m. tomorrow. It is very warm down the pit but fearful cold outside. It will be one of the worst Christmasses I have ever spent, last year's was bad enough at … France, but in Germany it's a washout altogether. I am properly fed up now with being a prisoner.

23rd Dec, Sun
Did not get up so early today as we are not at work. Did not do much but had a lot of falling-in. Was paid a couple of marks for two days' work, they keep one week on hand. Had to fall in for work at 10 p.m. I was at the same job, filling in the seams from where the coal has been got. Did not do a lot, being on my own for a great deal of the time. I was very sleepy and had stomach ache very bad. I don't like this shift at all, it loses so much of our sleeping time. Been a cold day but fine.

24th Dec, Mon
When we came up had a good wash. By the way, we get a bath every day, and need it, too! When I got back, had some soup and turned in. Had a good sleep till dinnertime then got up for some … soup (it wasn't soup for breakfast, it was coffee). During the evening, we fell in and had the Christmas tree lit. Later on, some of the Russians had a concert and, later, we were served out with a few biscuits, an apple and 10 cigarettes. I suppose this will be as much of a Christmas celebration as we shall see. Been a fine day, cold and frosty, ideal Christmas weather.

25th Dec, Tues, Christmas Day
Got up at nine or thereabouts, then had a drop of coffee and was messing about doing nothing in particular till dinnertime. For dinner, we had the same old soup, cabbage and turnips. After dinner was roll-call and we got our bread issue. Stagg and I bought some jam and had it to our bread. At night, we had some barley or, rather, wheat − similar to our English frumenty. It was a very fine day but cold. A more miserable Christmas we couldn't have had, I hope we are all well away in Blighty for next year's. I wonder what they are doing in England tonight?

26th Dec, Wed
Got up about 10 a.m., had some coffee and then, at 11 a.m., had some soup. Later, fell in for roll-call and was detailed off to work along with several more unloading some trucks of pit-props and such like. It was a very cold job, all the timber being frozen and heavy to lift. Got finished just before dark. Came back and got our bread issue and more soup and coffee. Turned in about 10 p.m., I am on afternoons down the pit tomorrow. I could just do with a parcel − or a letter from home. Been a fine day.

27th Dec, Thurs
Got up about eight. Had a dive for some potatoes as they brought them through where we sleep to take to the bakers for making bread – we had a good feed. Then got up about 10.30 a.m. and had a bowl of soup. At 2 p.m. went to work. I had a very nice job and a good fellow to work with. One of our poor fellows died this morning in the hospital. He had quinces and, with neglect, he died: the poor lad never had any food for four days. This is how the prisoners get done to, I call it murder. Fine day but cold.

28th Dec, Fri
Got up about ten, got some coffee and then a bowl of soup. At 2 p.m., went to work down the pit. I had a job amongst the stone and it wasn't such a hard job. Got finished in good time as the

engine which runs the trucks along had broken – so it was much easier for us. My word, but how weak we are, I cannot find enough strength to push an empty truck along now. Wish I could have a letter from home. Been a fine day.

29th Dec, Sat
Up about ten then got our issue of bread and had some coffee and soup, set off for the pit at 2 p.m. Stagg was on the same shift and, just as we were lined up to go down in the cage, he fell down in a kind of faint. He soon came round but he did not go down. My goodness, I expect to see half the poor lads laid up ill before long, the food is not sufficient for the work we have to do. How we are all longing for the packages to come through! Been a fine day again.

30th Dec, Sun
Got up about ten. Did not do much, no one was working today, but the lads who went on yesterday morning had to go on at night and so do a double shift. The poor kid who died the other day was buried today. I did not attend the funeral but several did. We are on morning shift next week so will have to be up in good time. I had a shave today or, rather, Stagg did it for me. He had one himself – I think he is a little better today but is a picture of ill health. Fine day, roll on peace!

31st Dec, Mon
Got up about 4 a.m. being on the morning shift this week, had some coffee and got myself ready for work and went to the pit. I had a very good job, only unloaded about five loads of stone then the shift was up. We had to come again at night as the pit is to be closed for New Year's Day. I was dead beat when I set off at about 9 p.m. We only got one very thin slice of bread to work on and I did not do very much, only unloaded two trucks of stone all night being too sleepy for work. This is an awful life! Been snowing today.

1st Jan, 1918, Tues

We got our bread issue as soon as we got in, so had some coffee and a bite, and I was so very tired that I turned in right away and slept till about eleven. I was that tired that I turned in again after soup at twelve, I won't call it dinner. Some of the lads had to go out working today and haven't got back yet, and this is nearly 9 p.m. Some of the Russians refused to work last night and so had to stand out in the snow all day without overcoats. What an awful New Year's Day!

2nd Jan, Wed

Got up at four. Warmed up a drop of soup then got some coffee and set off for the pit. Got the same old job shovelling stone but did not make myself sweat, emptied about six or so trucks. Went to work in my clogs today, they just about crippled me! Got a packet of writing paper and envelopes and sent a letter off to Florrie [Pickering]. I am feeling jolly hungry tonight, only had one small ladle of poor soup when we came off work at 2 p.m. Wish our parcel would come, we are nearly starved. Been thawing today, still a little snow on the ground.

3rd Jan, Thurs

Got up at four, warmed up some soup and got a bottle of coffee and then set off for the pit. I was on the same job. Did not get much sleep last night and, therefore, I was jolly well tired, going to sleep as I worked. There is very little to set down, all seems very quiet here. Stagg went sick again today but got 'duty'. I was feeling bad all day and the night previous, have a bad cold and sore throat. When we got back at dinnertime, we got some of the worst soup I've tasted, nothing but rotten beetroots, I couldn't eat any. This is how they treat the prisoners.

4th Jan, Fri

Got up at four, warmed up some soup, got some coffee and went to the pit. Had the same job but a little harder today. We heard a rumour that the English have agreed to come to terms now; I hope it's true as, goodness knows, we need it badly. Been a fine day but cold with a little snow a.m.

5th Jan, Sat
Up at 4 a.m., got ready and went to work. Had a very easy job this morning, only emptied about three trucks. My lamp kept going out so had to stay all the while with the fellow I was working with. We came again to do some work at 10 p.m. being our turn for the double shift. Cold, damp day. Got a small piece of bread for the extra shift, not nearly enough.

6th Jan, Sun
While we were waiting for the cage at the pit bottom, one of our fellows, Cassady – or Canada, as we call him – had a fight with one of the under-bosses, as he wanted to shift from the front of the ranks to the back. Nothing much happened today. Been fine but very cold. Got paid 6 marks today. We are longing to get our parcels up soon now. Someone had been round our beds and stolen the ration of bread we had issued for today while we were at work, this is a very dirty trick.

7th Jan, Mon
Cold and wet. I did not get up so early this morning as I am on the afternoon shift. We had our bread stolen while out at work last night or, rather, yesterday morning, so had none to take down with me. As we came up last night, one of the posterns started knocking one of our fellows about and nearly stunned him with his rifle because he did not get into 'fours' as soon as he came out of the cage. The postern who did it is the worst of the lot, a regular rotter.

8th Jan, Tues
Got up about 10.30 a.m. feeling very weak and ill. Had some soup then got ready for the pit. Went on the same job among the stone. Not much fresh news to report today. It was snowing as we came out and freezing all day.

9th Jan, Wed
Stagg was up in good time and warmed me some soup up about 8 a.m. I was up at eleven, had some soup, got ready for work and went down the pit. Got the same job but a trifle easier than yesterday. There is a strong rumour that the packages have arrived. I had my boots stolen by someone during the night so had to work in clogs, and nearly crippled me! Cold day.

10th Jan, Thurs
Got up at 10.30 a.m., had some soup at about twelve. Got ready and went to work. Was on a different job today, coal all the afternoon. When we came up at night it was raining and felt very cold. Nothing very important except that the list of names has arrived for the distribution of parcels, so things are looking brighter for us now.

11th Jan, Fri
Got up about 10 a.m. Stagg tried to get some potatoes when the sick went but lost his bowl in the bunch – however, he had it returned at dinnertime. Very poor soup today. Got ready and went to work. Been a very cold and snowy day. Nothing much to report on, regular slaves lives we are leading, same routine day in, day out; wished many a time I had been able to get back on the day I was captured.

12th Jan, Sat
Got up at 8 a.m. as I was going to pare some potatoes, but the Russians got there first so I did not have to go down. I got a postcard to say that my Swiss bread was on the way. Stagg got one to say that his toilet parcel was being sent. Went to work. Had a very good job along with one of our fellows. Found out later that the bread card was not for me but for another John Brough belonging to B Coy 2nd RMs. Strange, I have never seen nor heard of him before. Roll on peace!

13th Jan, Sun
Got up at 6 a.m. as Brown had the wind up about having to shift from our barrack to the place where the French have been upstairs – and what a mess it was in! It took us all day to get things straight. I got a bed next to my mate Stagg. It is much better than the other room. Been a fine day but cold yet I haven't been out much. I am on mornings next week. Wish the war was over. Feeling very weak and ill, may go sick tomorrow, my legs are very much swollen, don't know what is wrong with them.

14th Jan, Mon
Got up at 4 a.m., did not feel well so went sick. Turned in then for a few hours till it was time for the doctors. I got marked for hospital so got my things packed up ready but did not get off till about 3 p.m. Had a good bath then into a nice bed, and it was a treat, I can tell you! I don't know what is wrong with me except my legs are swollen.

15th Jan, Tues
I did not get up till half past eight and had breakfast – bread and coffee, but the bread was buttered, and went down well! They don't seem to be too badly fed here but are crowded out. I had an Italian in my bed, and lots of the others had two per bed. I am in a small room with four beds. All the Allies are represented here. Had an excellent dinner – soup, and macaroni and fruit – went down well, best I've had since being captured. Then had more bread and coffee about four o'clock. And for supper, had tea (sweetened) and two slices of bread and cheese with butter.

16th Jan, Wed
Got up about 8.30 a.m. Had a wash and made my bed then had breakfast – bread and coffee (milk in and butter on the bread). Afterwards, the doctor came round. Then I had a good sleep. I am feeling almost all right again now, the swellings have gone down on my legs. For dinner, we had a small bowl of soup – and jolly good

stuff, too – followed by a bowl of potatoes and a piece of meat with leeks, very good compared with the old barrack soups. For tea, we had coffee and bread and treacle. For supper, had a lovely bowl of thick soup followed by a heaped plate of potatoes and meat, or some such stuff, much better than at dinner.

17th Jan, Thurs
Got up about eight or so, made my bed and had a wash then had breakfast. It was very good – coffee and bread. Later on, the doctor came round. He did not examine me today but took a test of urine. Had a good sleep till dinner which was soup followed by a bowl of potatoes – very good, indeed, it made a fine dinner. I am feeling more like my old self again now. Had coffee and bread and butter for tea, one and a half slices per man, same as at breakfast. One more of our boys came in today, placed in the same room. For supper, had soup and potatoes with some kind of pickles, jolly good stuff, I had nearly two bowls full.

18th Jan, Fri
Got up about eight, made my bed, had a wash and got breakfast. I am feeling much better now. The swellings have all gone, suppose I shall be marked 'out' today, wish I was staying here for a good while, it's a jolly fine place. For dinner today had soup followed by pancake and a bowl of potatoes, same as we had last night. Very good soup with beans. White went to barracks today and one more Englishman came in. For tea, had coffee and bread and butter. Then for supper had two slices of bread and a good bowl of stewed prunes. I have been feeling very weak today, think I must have got a cold. Fine day.

19th Jan, Sat
Got up about eight, had a wash and made my bed then had breakfast of bread and butter with a bowl of coffee – very good – with milk. Later on, the doctor came round but did not say much. For dinner, had soup and a bowl of potatoes with cabbage … bean

soup. I am as full as can be, wish I was here for a good while then might get fat as the patients are very well fed here, almost as good as in an English hospital. One more of our fellows came in this morning, expect I shall be off soon as I am nearly right again now. After dinner, I had a good rest then, after tea, I got up and did some washing. We had a very good supper today, bean soup then a bowl of potatoes and cabbage, same as at dinnertime. I got an extra helping.

20th Jan, Sun

Got up about eight. Made my bed, then had a wash and had breakfast – coffee and bread and butter. I went with a Frenchman and two Russians to pare potatoes. We came on very well, one of the women brought us a sausage each and also some meat then, later on, a cup of soup and another good thick sausage. We were working on this job till dinner when we had soup and potatoes and cabbage with a bit of meat, pork it seemed like. For tea, had coffee, bread and butter. Then, for supper, bread and butter with a bowl of rice, nice and sweet. I am feeling tired tonight, been up all day.

21st Jan, Mon

Got up at 7.30 a.m., made my bed, had a wash and then breakfast of bread and coffee. Later, I turned in until the doctor had been round. Then the sister [RC nun] came for me to help the Russians paring potatoes. It was a very easy job, the potatoes being boiled and were nice and hot. Got a good bellyful and so did the others. Did not finish till dinnertime, had soup and potatoes with green beans. Later on, the sister again came for us to go on the potatoes, so we went. Did not do so badly, had a couple of sausages and coffee. This morning had a bit of bacon one of the Ruskies stole and shared out among us. Fine day.

22nd Jan, Tues

Got up about 8 a.m. Had a wash and made my bed then had breakfast of bread and coffee. Turned in till the doctor had been round then got up and went to pare potatoes, had about an hour doing this then it was dinnertime. Had bean soup and a plate of cold sago pudding and some red sauce. One more of our fellows has come here, he says the packets are up at the barracks. Wilson, one of the fellows in here, brought Cameron and I one of his tins of bully and so we had it to our soup at dinner. For tea, had coffee and bread and syrup. For supper, tea (sweet) and bread and pancakes. Cameron and I have to share a bed tonight. Been a very fine day.

23rd Jan, Wed
I did not sleep very well being hot with two in one bed. Got up and had a wash and breakfast – coffee and bread and butter. Later on, the doctor came round and marked several of us out including myself. Was down among the potatoes again. For dinner, had pea soup with a bowl of potatoes and turnips with barley, a very good dinner. For tea, coffee and bread and syrup. Brown brought my packet just as I was ready for off so had it to carry back. I have three days excused work. Only one packet for me but there is one coming among the French packets. Drew my clothes then had a jolly good tuck-in. Been a fine day.

24th Jan, Thurs
Got up about 9 a.m. I had to act as the orderly and clean up the room. There was a lot of paper and such like to clear out, refuse from the packets. The boys are quite happy now getting their packets through. I had a grocery parcel, drew it about three o'clock, did not know if it had been meant for me or not, belonging to the same regiment anyhow, and my emergency packet had been stopped, so felt bound to take it. Had a very good supper. Stagg and I are together again and so help one another with packets. Been a fine day.

25th Jan, Fri
Got up about 8 a.m. Cleared out the rubbish and such like from the floor. Boiled a bowl of potatoes and with some bully had a jolly

good dinner. After dinner, I had a sleep and then, about four o'clock, the old Jerry came and took me and several others on a fatigue unloading trucks of turnips. I am supposed to be doing no work for three days but it seems there is no rest here. I managed to get a pocketful of potatoes and they will come in useful tomorrow. We had a good supper tonight out of the parcel, the soup being uneatable today.

26th Jan, Sat
Got up about 8 a.m., had a bit of breakfast then swept out the room and such like. Stagg and I made a boiling of potatoes and, with a couple of tins of bully, had a lovely dinner. I did not do much during the afternoon. At night, I put some soup on and also made some cocoa for Stagg when he came off work at night. The packet is off down very well. We don't use much soup now and shall use less if we get our packets regularly. Been a fine day almost like summer. Hope to get a letter soon.

27th Jan, Sun
Got up at 8 a.m., had some breakfast and swept out the room. Stagg and I made ourselves some cocoa and also another lot of potatoes and they went down jolly fine with a little curry powder. Stagg's can had either boiled dry or one of the Russians had emptied out the water and spoiled the can and burned the potatoes. I see I am on the morning shift tomorrow. Been a very fine day. Stagg gave me a shave today. I also wrote a postcard to Hannah. Hope they are all well in the dear old homeland.

28th Jan, Mon
Got up at 4 a.m. Had some coffee and cold soup for breakfast. Did not take any bread down the pit as I had none to breakfast. Got a very decent job, the usual old thing stone packing. Did not work very hard, anyhow. The soup today was very poor, and worse at night. We got paid today, I did not get any as I have not been working during the last fortnight with being in hospital. We made

ourselves some more potatoes and had one of the tins of ham with them, went down well. Very fine day.

29th Jan, Tues
Got up at 4 a.m. Got ready and went to work. Was put on a job among the stone along with a youngster, had a very easy morning. When we came up, we were told that Burns, the chap in hospital with a bad chest, was dead, died this morning. This is the second Englishman. Brown was asking for subscriptions for a couple of wreaths for his funeral. Our packets has just about run out now, longing for the next issue. Been a very fine day.

30th Jan, Wed
Up at 4 a.m., put some soup on to warm up, then got ready and went to work. Was working on no. 10 flat – same old job on the stone but not such a hard day's work. When I came up in the after-noon, the list of regimental packets was up and I noticed my name was on several times. I think it is a mistake as there seems to be another man of the same name as myself but, if they mark my name off the emergency list, I shall feel like drawing the others. Been a very fine day.

31st Jan, Thurs
Got up at 4 a.m. Got some coffee and warmed up a drop of soup for breakfast then set off for work. Was on the same job at the same place. Had a very nice morning's work but was tired and hungry as we have finished off our packets now and have to rely on Jerry's soup. It was a little better at dinnertime but not half as good as the food we got in hospital. Been a very fine day.

1st Feb, Fri
Got up at 4 a.m. Warmed up some soup and filled our bottles with coffee then had breakfast and went to work. I was working on the same job, had a very good day's work. When we came off at the afternoon, Brown wanted several to go to Burns's funeral, only five

volunteered to go. Later, in the afternoon, the sergeant-major fell us all in and made us all go for a wash because of someone coming back [from the pit] without washing.

2nd Feb, Sat
Got up at 4 a.m. Warmed some soup and got our bottles filled with coffee, had breakfast and went to work. I had the same old job packing stone. There were nine packets came up in my name but, when we went to see them distributed, they were for the other Brough – five regimental and four bread packets. Worse luck, as our other packets are used now. There was no double shift today and I was jolly glad, as I don't know how we should have been able to stick it. Fine day.

3rd Feb, Sun
Did not get up till 10 a.m. when Stagg made a drop of cocca. Later on, had some soup – it was a little better today but not much. There has been no work at all today, we have had the day to ourselves. Lovely day, just like summer. After roll-call at 4 p.m., we got our bread and had a bowl of soup later on. Stagg has been busy today making a fresh brewing-up can and also shaving several of our fellows. Wonder how much longer the war is going to last ?

4th Feb, Mon
The old man came round waking us up at 4 a.m. I am on mornings again this week, worse luck. I got a half bowl of wheat left over from last night and it went down splendid but that was all we had, no coffee. This morning I have been working in a very low place in no.7. Not much to report on today. Been a lovely day, wish I could hear from home.

5th Feb, Tues
Got up at 4 a.m. Put some soup on to warm then got some coffee and had breakfast. Went to work. Was on the same old job, stone packing in no.9. Been a fine day. Longing for another packet as the

other is finished now. We had very good soup at dinnertime, considering, but not up to much at night. All seems very quiet here, someone was saying they [the German miners] were coming out on strike, but nothing has happened as yet, worse luck.

6th Feb, Wed
Got up at 4 a.m. Put some soup on to warm and got some coffee then went to work. I was, first of all, sent to no.10, then found there was no work there so came to no.9, and found it the same. Had a good rest along an old working and had a sleep, then went to no.7 and had a very good job for the remainder of the shift. When we came up tonight, found the list of names had arrived for the packets. My name was not on but shall draw Burns's instead, the fellow who died last week. Dull day.

7th Feb, Thurs
Got up at 4 a.m. Warmed up a bowl of soup, got a bottle of coffee and went to work. Was working on no.9, had a good day's carbide[?]. When we got back, had a drop of very decent soup for dinner – but it was not at all good for supper! Been a rather wet, cold day. Nothing very much to report today, still hoping for the packets to come soon. What a miserable life it is, we are nothing but slaves. Don't we all long for peace and getting back to dear old Blighty!

8th Feb, Fri
Up at usual time, warmed a bowl of soup, got a bottle of coffee and off to work. Was working on no.8 today, had a very easy time. It was clearing away some stone from a fall of roofing. I am feeling very weak now with only the German food to live on which is not at all good at its best. Today, the soup was not half so good and the rations of bread were only small and very brown, about 2 inches thick for the day. It has been a dull, wet day. Still no packets are up and we are losing hope of getting them at all.

9th Feb, Sat
Got up at 4 a.m. Warmed up some soup and got some coffee then went to work. Was sent to no.8, had a very easy morning. It was a rather dull, cold day, inclined to rain. We are still in hopes of the packets arriving but, as yet, nothing has been heard. There was a double shift on tonight, so had a bit of sleep during the afternoon then got a double ration and went to work again at 10 p.m. Had a very easy time, only did three trucks of stone at no.9.

10th Feb, Sun
Got up about twelve in time for soup, it was hardly worth going down to draw. During the afternoon, we got paid for the last week of December. I got 6 marks so bought a few biscuits at the canteen. For tea, we had barley and it was very good, I managed to get a second helping. Some of the boys have been having a straightening up with Brown over the dirty tricks he has been doing on us all – think he will be leaving soon as everyone is fed up with him. Been a cold day.

11th Feb, Mon
I did not get up till 10 a.m. then went and helped to empty the latrine buckets. Came back and got some very poor soup. Got ready and went to work. I am on the 2 p.m. shift this week. Not much to report today, in fact, I have let the diary get too far back to remember. Stagg is on the same shift as me.

12th Feb, Tues to 17th Feb, Sun
[No entries made.]

18th Feb, Mon
Stagg was very sick this week, had three or four days off. He seems to be properly run down and had diarrhoea very bad. I was on mornings this week. Nothing much to report.

19th Feb, Tues to 22nd Feb, Fri
[No entries made.]

23rd Feb, Sat
Got up at 4 a.m., had a little breakfast then went to work. There was a double shift on today so I happened to get it but had an easy time. Was on coal during the extra shift, only did five wagons. I have a very sore finger, think I must have got it poisoned.

24th Feb, Sun
Was feeling more dead than alive today and had a very painful hand. It is the right hand, too, so found a great difficulty in writing a post-card. Not much to report.

25th Feb, Mon
Went sick with my finger but was too late to go to the doctor's so the corporal put me in revere along with Allan, an Irishman, who also had a bad finger. Stagg went sick as well but had to go to work. I am on afternoon shift this week.

26th Feb, Tues
Got up and went to the doctor's and he lanced my finger – and didn't half give me some pain! I stayed in revere again all day, rather dreary place but better than work. My finger … and giving a good deal of pain.

27th Feb, Wed
The corporal in charge of the revere sent me to hospital when he came to do the dressings. So got ready and went, and was glad to get there. There is only one other Englishman here.

28th Feb, Thurs
This morning, I had my hand operated on. They gave me some chloroform so I did not feel the pain much. It was not as bad as I expected it would have been. When I awoke, I was all bandaged up and feeling a little better.

1st Mar, 1918, Fri

The sister gave me some pain last night and also this morning when she dressed my hand. I am allowed up all day. Sleep along with the Englishman from our barracks, Chubb is his name. By the way, he is a Canadian!

2nd Mar, Sat

The doctor had me on the table again this morning and had another operation. This time I did not feel any pain at all. When the sister dressed it on Sunday, I noticed that he had cut a hole through from the front to the back of the hand and stuffed some gauze in to drain out the poison. Feeling a bit sore again now. Brown was up with three regimental packets for me and two breads and also one clothing packet consisting of one greatcoat and one kit-bag.

3rd Mar, Sun to 14th Mar, Thurs

[No entries made. He remained in hospital.]

15th Mar, Fri

Brown was down today with the lists for us to sign. He had brought the packets down but did not serve them out as the corporal was out for the weekend, or something or other, so is coming down on Monday to serve them out. Sent Stagg a tin of tobacco back with Brown. Nothing very much to report.

16th Mar, Sat and 17th Mar, Sun

[No entries made.]

18th Mar, Mon

Stagg and Brown came down today and brought the packets. There was only bread for me this time – two packets of Copenhagen bread and they were very mouldy. Stagg has got a photo of his wife and child – but he doesn't look too well himself. He brought me a couple of cigars so had a smoke during the afternoon. Not much to report.

19th Mar, Tues to 24th Mar, Sun
[No entries made.]

25th Mar, Mon
Brown came down and brought some packets along or, rather, the other fellows did, as Brown had a bad leg or something. Stagg sent down a packet containing 1 pr boots, 1 pr shoes, 1 cap and 3 pocket-handkerchiefs; also, some fags and one loaf of bread. He sent a note to say that all my packets were clothing this time so sent one of his breads, a Swiss loaf. Suppose there is some more clothing up at the barrack for me. I am glad I have got some boots to work in as it was awkward in clogs.

26th Mar, Tues and 27th Mar, Wed
[No entries made.]

28th Mar, Thurs
I sent some soup squares up for Stagg with the Australian who was sharing the same bed as me in the hospital. Also sent a note to say he was not to send any more clothes down here as I have quite enough now to carry back and expect to be out soon now. There is still one of our men left so I am not quite on my own. He is a very nice fellow, a Scottish man, by the way. I had the bed to myself tonight. The doctor has not been today.

29th Mar, Fri
The doctor did not come today. We had macaroni and soup for dinner. At night, we got pancakes. There was plenty of food today and we got extras. Been a rather wild sort of day – just like March – and also thunder and high winds. The parson was in this evening and told us that the Germans had taken 45,000 English prisoners during the recent advance but I am not believing it.

30th Mar, Sun
[No entry.]

31st Mar, Sun

This morning, J. Campbell [the Scotsman] and I had a good breakfast – he opened a tin of bacon and I opened some jam and milk. Then, when the coffee came along, there was a great square of cake and the usual slice of bread and butter. For dinner, had meat and soup and apple jam, also custard – a three course dinner, the best since I arrived here. Wrote a letter to Mrs Baker of Whitby, also postcard to Leeds. For tea, had chocolate and more cake and bread and butter and, for supper, cocoa and bread. At night, Campbell opened a packet of oatcakes and we ate them to jam and margarine. Got properly full tonight and thought that, if it is Easter, we had not half celebrated the event! The church bells have been ringing all day and it seems a big day with them all here. On Saturday night, we had coloured … for supper, mine was a bright red one and Campbell's a green. We don't know much here but think it must be Easter or something.

[It was, as he thought, Easter Sunday]

1st Apr, 1918, Mon

This morning, we had a tin of bloaters between us and also a drop of milk in the coffee and had a jolly good feed. It seems to be a general holiday in Germany today, bells have been ringing all day. For dinner, had soup and potatoes and meat. For tea, coffee and bread and butter and with one piece of cake and, for supper, tea – very weak – and two slices of bread with some kind of paste. Campbell opened one tin of … The sister came in with a great tale that Paris was in the hands of the Germans, we did not believe it.

2nd Apr, Tues

After a fairly good night's sleep got up about seven. Had a wash and had breakfast. Had the ordinary diet today, the high feeding seems over. The doctor came today, the military doctor, and he marked a good many for the lagers. For dinner, had soup and a bowl of potatoes and sauerkraut. At 3 p.m., the usual bread and jam and coffee. For supper, had a bowl of barley and piece of sausage extra tonight, plenty and very good, too. Been a dull day. I am still going strong but expect to be marked out soon now, just Jock and I of the 'Englanders' left here.

3rd Apr, Wed
After a fairly good night's sleep got up at about half past seven. Had a wash and made my bed, then Campbell opened a tin of herrings for breakfast and, my, they were salty but we managed to finish them off. The usual breakfast then the old doctor came round, first for a fortnight, he did not say much. For dinner, had soup and a basin of carrots. For tea, the usual bread and jam and, for supper, had bread and butter and two bowls of pea soup. Later, Campbell and I had a packet of biscuits and jam, feeling full up. They have been clearing the men out of the wards below to make room for some wounded soldiers. Those going to the lagers went out before dinner. Fine day with showers.

4th Apr, Thurs
Got up about half past seven, made my bed and had a wash. Had breakfast, coffee and bread and butter. I opened a tin of milk for our coffee and had white bread and jam – our stock of tinned food and bread is fast running out. The old doctor was round later on. For dinner, had soup, and carrots and potatoes with small pieces of meat. The usual bread and jam for two o'clock and, for supper, had black peas and bowl full of pieces of sausage, plenty of it. A good many wounded German soldiers arrived today, I saw them when I went to get my finger dressed. Been a fine day. The old doctor came round about 8 p.m. and inspected a lot of us. I have an Italian sleeping with me tonight.

5th Apr, Fri
Got up at half past six. Made the bed and had a wash, then Campbell opened a tin of partridge paste and we had it for breakfast. I have finished off my white bread now so am looking forward to the next wagon to come up. For dinner, had basin of soup and cold

potatoes with some sour sauce on them and also custard, plenty of extras. One more Englishman came and brought me two letters, one from Mrs Baker and one from Jennie [his married sister Jane]. Had the usual for tea and, for supper, had bread and butter with pancakes and a bowl of quaker oats or something very similar, plenty of extras. Been a fine day.

6th Apr, Sat
Got up at 6.30 a.m., made my bed and had a wash then had breakfast, the usual bread and butter and coffee. Had a thorough clean out of the rooms and the doctor came round and all was good. For dinner, had soup and a bowl of potatoes and carrots and some oatmeal stuffing. For tea, bread and jam and coffee. For supper, had black peas, plenty of them but very weak. We got one more Russian in today and have three Englishmen all told, one came in yesterday. Expect I shall be out next week as they are getting full up again now. One more Russian came in at night. It has been a fine day.

7th Apr, Sun
Got up about seven, had a wash and made my bed. Had breakfast – Campbell opened a tin of sausages and we all three had a good meal. For dinner, we had soup and potatoes and cabbage with a piece of meat. Then had an hour's sleep. At 2 o'clock, had chocolate made by the French, Campbell gave a tin of cocoa for it. Fine, too, it was and we had a packet of biscuits and jam to it with the bread and butter. Two Russians came in today and we are almost full up again now. For supper, had two slices of bread and sausage-meat and a bowl of thin macaroni soup, very nice and sweet. I used a tin of beans for supper. Wrote a letter to Mrs Baker.

8th Apr, Mon and 9th Apr, Tues
[No entries made.]

10th Apr, Wed
Woke up this morning with the priest coming in to a service over

130

the Belgium who is very ill. Had the usual breakfast then the doctor came round. Later, had dinner which consisted of cabbage and potatoes, almost like barrack soup. For tea, the same and, for supper, weak barley. 'Collie' opened a pot of lemon curd and we had it to some bread, very nice. The Belgian died this morning about eleven. Got no more patients in today. Been a fine day. Not much to report today. The sister has been too busy to do any dressings today.

11th Apr, Thurs
Got up at half past seven, had a wash then breakfast. 'Collie' opened a tin of veal loaf and we had it to some white bread. With the issue of German bread and butter made it a good breakfast. The sister was right busy dressing the patients and cleaning up the wards for the military doctor is coming round. He arrived just after dinner, he did not say much, none are marked out. For dinner, had weak soup and bowl of potatoes and beans and carrots, very nice. The usual tea. For supper, had macaroni soup and a bowl of potatoes. Later, we had biscuits and lemon curd. Also had a plate of oat-cakes. Dull day.

12th Apr, Fri
Got up about half past seven after rather a sleepless night with toothache. 'Collie' opened a tin of veal loaf and we had a good breakfast. Later on, the doctor came round and marked me Fredrichesfield, much to my surprise, and also marked Campbell barrack. For dinner, had soup and a bowl of potatoes and green beans. For tea, the usual. Later on, had a packet of oat-cakes and butter. For supper, had a bowl of tea, bread and pancakes. Later, had some bread and sardines. Been a fine day. Suppose we shall not sleep much tomorrow night among the bugs!

13th Apr, Sat
Got up about half past six and packed my boxes ready for the barrack then had breakfast. 'Collie' opened up a tin of herrings and

we had some white bread to it making an excellent breakfast. The Belgian was buried this morning. He had a fine funeral, band and all. The postern came about ten and we got our clothes and set off. Found the boys looking much better since their packets have come. Stagg is out of revere and he made an excellent dinner. Later on, had a game at cards. I was glad we had got off work down the pit for a time. Anyhow, hope I never see it again! I am feeling lost here after being in hospital.

14th Apr, Sun
Got up or, at least, was kept up by the bugs – they simply rolled out in thousands – so Campbell and I walked about all night. I went to the pictures along with some more of the fellows. They were very good but I was tired with the walk as I put my new clothes on and the boots were very stiff. At night, the boys had a concert and it was very good, some rather good turns. I did not sleep much during the night, the bugs were too busy. Fine day, not much to report.

15th Apr, Mon
Got up and had a snack then turned in for a few hours as the bugs don't bite so much in the light. Stagg is the orderly man this week so had to help him with the cooking. I did not get to Fredrichesfield today, haven't heard any more about it. I made my bed down on the floor tonight and had a better sleep. I wish I was back in the old hospital again. Campbell went to work this morning but is going sick again tomorrow. Fine day, not much news.

16th Apr, Tues
I got up about ten having had a much better sleep last night. Stagg was busy cleaning the windows today. The packet wagon came up today and was unloaded during the afternoon. None of the English draw any soup now as they are all getting packets through. For dinner, we made some tea and a tin of salmon and enjoyed it well.

Had a good play of cards this afternoon. I don't mind staying here a bit longer only they don't send me down [the pit] again. The boys were paid out today. Been a fine day.

[No more daily entries are made, the diary concludes:]

I did not keep the diary being too idle.

Just a few days at the commando then went to Fredrichesfield and had five weeks there. Had a good time there, did no work. Then got sent to a commando being marked … Lager. Thought we should have got an easy job but found we were out from seven in the morning till nine o'clock at night on market-gardening at Hamm outside Dusseldorf. Get all our food at the house where I work, plenty of it, but the hours are too long and the barrack is a small place and far too over-crowded. Came here on 29th May, had a holiday the next day, then two days' work (which seemed like two weeks) and was paid 60 pfennigs each. Everyone works here, of course. We get Sunday off – and need it, too! We get five meals a day – and need them, too! It would be a good commando were we finished at six each night, but nine o'clock is too long. My boss is a market-gardener and so are most around here. I am taking my washing there tomorrow, Monday, 3rd June.

[Final note is entered as below:]

Left for Fredrichesfield on Tuesday about noon, 19th November, 1918, [en route] for England. When we got there, we were issued with four packets each, one biscuits and three groceries, so had a very good evening. The old camp is not at all like it used to be, the gardens are now bonfire places with all the packet cases. We did not get much sleep during the night and we moved off next day about nine o'clock. With a few changes and so forth we arrived in Holland about half past two, then had a good long march to our destination, a school. Did not go out much at night.

[On the opposite page to the above is entered:]

Private J. Brough 382 RMLI,
2nd Batt. Royal Marine Light Inf.,
Gefangeneu Lager,
Wahn,
Deutschland.
Kriegsgefangeneupost